RMJM **INSIDE OUT
OUTSIDE IN**

black dog
publishing

RM

JM

CONTENTS

8

INTRODUCTION
PAUL STALLAN, UK DESIGN DIRECTOR

An anniversary is a time for both celebration and reflection – and 50 years is certainly a landmark for any architectural firm.

In simple terms, RMJM is a UK-based, design-led architectural practice with an ambitious international outlook; we have ten offices and more than 600 staff. But such a statement can only, of course, hint at the strength of character and the depth of experience within the firm.

Our work can – and does – speak for itself so the purpose of *Inside Out, Outside In* extends well beyond that of a monograph. It provides an insight into the dynamic that is RMJM.

In these pages, we hope to demonstrate that a large, international practice can be responsive, flexible, innovative and passionate. That it can promote individual creativity and project enterprise; all we ask of our team is that they achieve design excellence. At RMJM, we believe in the process of design and have a genuine appetite, sensitivity and capability to work on projects of any scale and complexity.

In this book, we show how the firm's philosophy has been instrumental to our success – a philosophy that was clear from that very first day when two committed, vastly different characters came together to promulgate their vision of what architecture could achieve. These founding partners would leave a distinctive legacy to UK architecture, with an approach that looked as much at people as it did at buildings. A partnership of some very real substance, it gave us the platform to progress and expand in dynamic fashion.

In this book, too, we see how our philosophy has been translated across our ten offices, with a look at the culture of our people and the architecture they produce. We have cut RMJM in half to reveal our workings and methods. We describe our culture as one that values and places emphasis on process, the processes of working and sharing, of teamwork and generosity. RMJM is an architectural practice that promotes a collaborative design approach, offering clients an opportunity to actively partner and develop bespoke design solutions so that a project achieves its maximum potential. I believe people will be genuinely surprised at the range and type of work that the practice is presently working on, from the small scale to the super scale and across a wide range of industry sectors. The book focuses primarily on our work in the UK but it also profiles a selection of projects from across the globe.

'Design is a conversation.'

If *Inside Out, Outside In* is to leave a single message it is this: 'process over product'. We are a multi-disciplinary practice with a business model that is neither stack 'em high and sell 'em cheap, nor niche and narrow-focused. Our practice embodies an intellectually challenging message. About the beauty of working creatively, of blending different skills and different viewpoints to deliver something that is about more than architecture. We live in a commercial world, so our design-led approach also encompasses a full understanding of the whole procurement process. We're as keen to unlock value as our clients are. The ability to secure the best project work and surpass the expectations of our clients depends on the quality of our differentiated design thinking and our ability to stimulate constructive dialogue throughout the life of a project.

RMJM's work goes deep into the specifics of a project – the client, climate, culture, the economies and the social and political issues – wherever we are working. We are mature and serious in our pursuit of a design ethic that takes full cognisance of the unique nature of every project; that remains sensitive to the brief – and brings life to it. We want to work with our clients to imagine the very best architecture we can. In 50 years, our commitment to the principles of modernism, and our belief in the human dimension has never wavered.

HISTORY

IT'S NOT AT ALL OBVIOUS WHY ROBERT MATTHEW AND STIRRAT JOHNSON-MARSHALL WENT INTO PARTNERSHIP.

56

"Robert would come down on the Friday night sleeper from Edinburgh, work all weekend and head back on the Sunday night. We would come in on the Monday to find a plethora of notes and sketches about the various projects we were working on."
Ken Feakes, Partner 1972 – 1985, Director 1985 – 1989,
Project Architect, New Zealand House

"Stirrat was very good at being the 'devil's advocate'. He made you question your own work, always bringing it back to the client: how is it going to work for them? He was very generous in his praise."
Sir Andrew Derbyshire,
Chairman 1983 – 1989, President 1989 – 1998

A partnership should be a meeting of minds, a coming together of vision and ambition. It need not be a fusion of personalities. Which is just as well. Formed in 1956, RMJM was Robert Matthew and Stirrat Johnson-Marshall. Robert so blunt; Stirrat quietly encouraging. One a traditionalist, focused on design and construction, the other immersed in systems and planning. Perhaps it's just as well that their offices were separated by 500 miles.

What they did share, however, was a belief in humane modernism; architecture as service. With public sector backgrounds – Robert as former Chief Architect to the Scottish Office and later London County Council, and Stirrat Chief Architect to the Ministry of Education – it was no surprise that the practice flourished on commissions for schools, universities and hospitals. And it was to be another public commission – albeit from overseas – that would propel the firm to prominence.

The 15-storey New Zealand House has been described as "London's most distinguished 1960s office block". Now a Grade II listed building, it was commissioned by the New Zealand government as that country's official face in Great Britain. A team of 12, including a number of native New Zealanders fresh off the boat at Tilbury, worked on a project that would become an eloquent expression of RMJM's belief in connectivity. From the innovative glazing systems right down to the door handles and even the crockery, the attention to detail was breathtaking and would set the tone for the work to follow.

62

NEW ZEALAND HOUSE, LONDON

With offices in Edinburgh and London, RMJM was described as a federation of semi-autonomous groups, each one developing its own distinct strategy, albeit within Robert and Stirrat's distinctive human dimension. A strong public ethos is not without its problems, however. By the late 1980s, RMJM had stagnated, a victim of its stubborn belief in homogeneous design, a philosophy totally at odds with a commercial client-base more interested in returns than in good architecture. While others rushed to riches, RMJM went round in somewhat introspective circles.

The early 90s were a turning point. An injection of fresh young talent and a resurgence in higher education spending invigorated the firm and, suddenly, RMJM was getting interesting and important new designs built again. Today, with offices across the globe, the firm has found a way to harmonise the human aesthetic with the profit margin, creating buildings of strength and character, of their time and place. Were Robert and Stirrat alive, they would undoubtedly recognise the firm that bears their names. Marked by innovation, connectivity and a certain bloody-mindedness, RMJM has always been about more than architecture.

62

COMMONWEALTH INSTITUTE, LONDON

66

UNIVERSITY OF YORK

68

COCKENZIE POWER STATION, EAST LOTHIAN

69

ROYAL COMMONWEALTH POOL, EDINBURGH

69

UNIVERSITY OF BATH

69

CZECHOSLOVAKIAN EMBASSY, LONDON

71

LOCAL EXAMINATIONS SYNDICATE, CAMBRIDGE

74

NINEWELLS HOSPITAL, DUNDEE

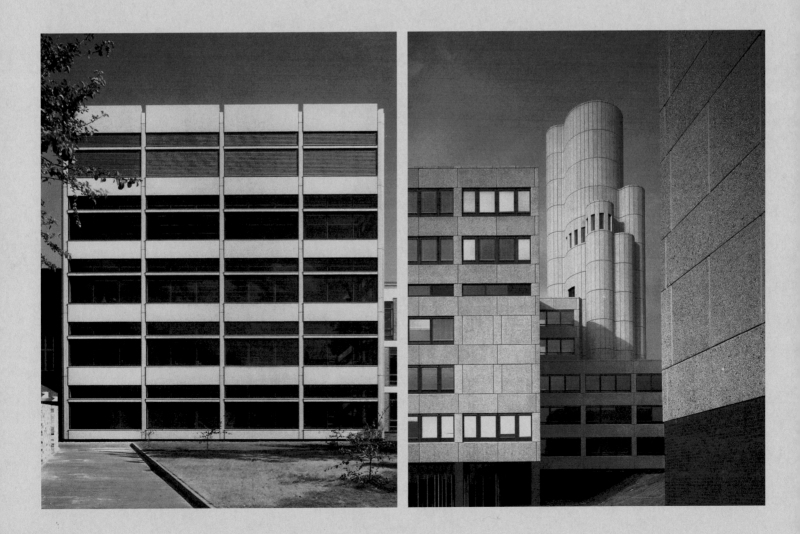

THE 1970s AND 80s WERE, IT MUST BE SAID, NOT KIND
TO MODERNIST PRACTICES LIKE RMJM. MODERNISM
HAD FALLEN SERIOUSLY OUT OF FASHION, DUE IN
NO SMALL PART TO THE GLUT OF POOR QUALITY,
POORLY PLANNED BUILDINGS THROWN UP BY THE
UNSCRUPULOUS DURING THE 60s. NOSTALGIA WAS
IN. AND WORSE WAS TO COME.

The acquisitive culture of the 1980s heralded an era of
architectural timidity; money talked and good design all
too often fell silent. RMJM found it hard to adapt and,
consequently, the firm's buildings of the period were not
particularly memorable (with one or two exceptions, of
course). RMJM wasn't alone; many progressive firms
struggled to make sense of the prevailing culture, but the
practice's history and, certainly, its philosophy left it at a
significant disadvantage. However, this period did see the
expansion of RMJM's overseas work thanks to an early
presence in Africa, the Middle East and south-east Asia.

History is there to be learned from – not ignored. And today's
international success is testament to the firm's ability to do
just that.

74

UNIVERSITY OF STIRLING

84

DISTILLERS HOUSE, EDINBURGH

95

UNIVERSITY OF LINCOLN

98

THE TRON THEATRE, GLASGOW

01

UNIVERSITY OF CAMBRIDGE

02

FALKIRK WHEEL

03

UNIVERSITY OF HERTFORDSHIRE

04

CHEMISTRY RESEARCH LABORATORY, UNIVERSITY OF OXFORD

05

GLASGOW HARBOUR

06

NEWCASTLE COLLEGE

THERE'S A HARMONY IN DIVERSITY.

600 people. 46 nationalities. 54 languages. All brought together in ten offices. Each with the founding partners' commitment to human modernism. Each with an overriding belief in connectivity. But within this coherent whole lies a beating heart of diversity. With such a young, dynamic team it could hardly be any other way.

RMJM may be 50 years old. But it feels much younger. From Stirrat's encouraging hand, to the firm's revitalisation in the early 90s and on to the present day, youth has been no barrier to success at RMJM. In 2006, the average age of our directors and associates is 40. If you've got the ideas, you'll get a chance to put them into practice here.

Each individual office has its own working process. Partly this is driven by sensitivity to the culture of the country in which it's based – a culture that is reflected in every design created by RMJM. But it's also down to the personality of the people who work there. RMJM creates a platform for creative thought, an opportunity for personal expression; this is meritocracy in action.

RMJM has grown by intuition, not by grand ambition. By commitment to design, not by politicking or grandstanding. Our success is the product of every one of those 600 individuals – and despite the formidable reputations of our founding partners, it has always been thus. From Robert and Stirrat onwards, the design leadership shown by each director has created an environment in which only the best designs make the transition from page to site.

There's a feeling of inclusion across all of RMJM's offices. An atmosphere of collaboration. Although there is no signature RMJM building, there is a consistency in approach, born out of a collective passion for architecture and design. Harmony through diversity, as this section shows us.

08:24

09:24

13:13

11:22

MARIJN HONG KONG
JOURNEY TO WORK
VIEW AT WORK
TYPICAL LUNCH
MY DESK

08:55

13:25

15:50

11:50

07:40

13:21

14:32

14:57

08:45

11:00

13:30

18:15

WHAT IS YOUR FAVOURITE?
ARTWORK
BOOK
FILM
FOOD
DRINK (WHILST AT WORK)

CLAIRE EDINBURGH
LIBERTY GUIDING THE PEOPLE,
EUGÈNE DELACROIX
A MOVEABLE FEAST, ERNEST HEMINGWAY
AMÉLIE
DOUGHNUTS
CHINESE GREEN TEA

COLIN LONDON
THE WEATHER PROJECT, OLAFUR ELIASSON

DR STRANGELOVE
SHISH TAOUK
WATER

DANA CAMBRIDGE
THE BLUE ROOM, SUZANNE VALADON
FULL COLLECTION OF ASTERIX & OBELIX
(FRENCH VERSION)
AMADEUS
DIM SUM & LEBANESE
ROOM TEMPERATURE WATER

GRAHAM LONDON
FIVE ANGELS FOR THE MILLENNIUM, BILL VIOLA
THE LAST TEMPTATION, NIKOS KAZANTZAKES
DIVA
LEBANESE
WHITE COFFEE

MIKE HONG KONG
CUT-AWAY DIAGRAMS FROM THE
HAYNES MANUAL COVERS
CATCH 22, JOSEPH HELLER
TO SIR WITH LOVE
STEAMED BEEF AND SUET PUDDING,
MASH, PEAS AND GRAVY
LATTE WITH SPRINKLING OF RAW SUGAR
ON THE TOP

ADAM CAMBRIDGE
EIGHT TORQUED ELLIPSES, RICHARD SERRA
CATCH 22, JOSEPH HELLER
PULP FICTION
PASTA WITH TOMATO SAUCE
WATER

ALICIA GLASGOW
SWANS REFLECTING ELEPHANTS, SALVADOR DALI
ATLAS OF THE WORLD
SOYLENT GREEN
ORGANIC
WEAK MILKY TEA WITH TWO SUGARS

SILVIA LONDON
BLUE, YVES KLEIN
BRAVE NEW WORLD, ALDOUS HUXLEY
THE MATRIX
SUSHI
STRONG WHITE COFFEE

ALASTAIR GLASGOW
CHRIST OF SAINT JOHN OF THE CROSS,
SALVADOR DALI
THE PARA HANDY TALES, NEIL MUNRO
CITIZEN KANE
LAYERED CASHEW NUT AND MUSHROOM ROAST
TEA

SUNNY BEIJING
SUNFLOWERS, VINCENT VAN GOGH
STONE STORY
GONE WITH THE WIND
SI CHUAN
DIET COKE

SHELLEY EDINBURGH
THE BROKEN COLUMN, FRIDA KAHLO
SEXING THE CHERRY, JEANETTE WINTERSON
DIRTY DANCING
GREEN THAI CURRY
GREEN TEA

ANA MARIE DUBAI
THE LAST SUPPER, LEONARDO DA VINCI
THE ALCHEMIST, PAOLO COELHO
MEET JOE BLACK
PASTA OR JAPANESE
WATER OR JUICE

SIMON EDINBURGH
AFTER LUNCH, PATRICK CAULFIELD
THE THIRTY-NINE STEPS, JOHN BUCHAN
LE MANS
CONFIT DE CANARD
TEA

ZHAO BEIJING
SURREALIST ANGEL
MONKEY KING
STAR WARS
HOT POT
TEA

MIKE LONDON
THE WORK OF ANDY GOLDSWORTHY
THE THIRD POLICEMAN, FLANN O'BRIEN
THE GODFATHER
SALAD
WHITE COFFEE, NO SUGAR

EIRINI CAMBRIDGE
TENDING (BLUE), JAMES TURRELL
THE LAST TEMPTATION, NIKOS KAZANTZAKES
ROCCO AND HIS BROTHERS
BAKED HERB SALMON WITH ROASTED
VEGETABLE AND VIRGIN OLIVE OIL
ORGANIC EARL GREY TEA WITH
SEMI-SKIMMED MILK

ERICA GLASGOW
THE STEERAGE, ALFRED STIEGLITZ
THE KITE RUNNER, KHALED HOSSEINI
AMERICAN BEAUTY
SUSHI
TEA WITH MILK

SUCHERA BANGKOK
TREES
ART 4D
SHUTTER
PAPAYA SALAD
HOT CHOCOLATE

MARILYN DUBAI
SUNFLOWERS, VINCENT VAN GOGH
MEMOIRS OF A GEISHA, ARTHUR GOLDEN
DANCER IN THE DARK
LASAGNA COOKED BY MY MUM
POWDER CAFÉ AND SUGAR!

MARIJN HONG KONG
ANTARCTIC UNITS, JOEP VAN LIESHOUT
TOUCHING THE VOID, JOE SIMPSON
BLADERUNNER
BITTERBALLEN
ONE SHOT OF STRONG COFFEE WITH
TWO SHOTS OF FOAMY MILK

DAVID EDINBURGH
ANY DRAWING BY ELIA HAMILTON
(AGED TWO AND A HALF)
DON CAMILLO TAKES THE DEVIL BY THE TAIL,
GIOVANNI GUARESCHI
YANKEE DOODLE DANDY
PEPPERONI PIZZA WITH ANCHOVIES AND OLIVES
WHITE (FAIRTRADE) COFFEE, ONE SUGAR

EUGENE DUBAI
THE ARNOLFINI MARRIAGE, JAN VAN EYCK
THE DA VINCI CODE, DAN BROWN
RAVENOUS
CHICKEN KORMA
WHITE COFFEE, TWO SUGARS

MARIA ANTONIA SINGAPORE
AN ARTISTIC SCULPTURE OF A NUDE LADY AND
THE WORKS OF ANTONIO GAUDI
THE ALCHEMIST, PAULO COELHO
BRAVEHEART
SPAGHETTI WITH TOMATO SAUCE, MINCED MEAT
AND MUSHROOMS
HOT CHOCOLATE/WATER

NATHAN EDINBURGH
UNTITLED (NOVELS), RACHEL WHITEREAD
MY CENTURY, GUNTHER GRASS
THE DELICATESSEN
FILLET OF BEEF
MILKY BUILDER (STRONG TEA, LOTS OF MILK)

NATALIE EDINBURGH
THE SNAIL, MATISSE
EVENING CLASS, MAEVE BINCHY
PRETTY WOMAN
CHOCOLATE
HOT CHOCOLATE

PAUL EDINBURGH
ST PETER'S BASILICA
THE SCOTTISH ENLIGHTENMENT
2001 A SPACE ODYSSEY
ANYTHING JAPANESE
WHITE COFFEE

TIAN FU BEIJING
FATHER
THE COLLECTIONS OF MAO ZEDONG
E.T.
SEAFOOD
WATER

SRI SINGAPORE
MICHELANGELO'S DAVID

CHARLIE AND THE CHOCOLATE FACTORY
CHICKEN RICE
WHITE COFFEE

AMY EDINBURGH
DOMAIN FIELD, ANTONY GORMLEY
HARRY POTTER (WHOLE COLLECTION)
PRIDE & PREJUDICE (BBC VERSION)
MASHED POTATO
TEA, MEDIUM STRENGTH, SKIMMED MILK

LOUIS BEIJING
BOTANY
MONKEY KING
THE LORD OF THE RINGS
HOT POT
COFFEE WITH ONE SUGAR

VAN DUBAI
THE CRUCIFIX
THE HOLY BIBLE
THE NOTEBOOK
EGG MISSUA
HERBAL TEA

FLORENCE HONG KONG
THE KISS, AUGUST RODIN
THE LITTLE PRINCE, ANTOINE DE SAINT-EXUPERY
SOMEWHERE IN TIME
FOIE GRAS
WHITE COFFEE, ONE SUGAR

JOURNEY   LUNCH

VIEW   DESK

PROCESS

ARCHITECTURE THAT HAS LESS
TO DO WITH FORMS THAN FORMS
OF EXPERIENCE.

A building is an experience. A living, breathing entity that shapes our lives, colours our thinking, enhances our existence. It speaks for us all; therefore, it needs to listen to what is being said. To the landscape, to the people. To history and the future. And then it needs to make sense of it all. A coherent summation of every influence.

RMJM has always been concerned with connectivity. Connections between architecture, engineering and art. Connections between the built and the green environment. And the connections forged between the people we work with. Architects are only one function within RMJM. We're a firm of planners, engineers, interior designers and landscape architects. It's a holistic philosophy and this, as much as anything can, defines our approach to architecture. For Robert Matthew and Stirrat Johnson-Marshall, this collaboration might not have been easy. In fact, it was often anything but. A battle of minds, however, need not create a war. Rather, it fights complacency. Challenges conceptions. And makes victors of the client.

There's a generosity in collaboration. After all, we may not have all the answers.

By questioning our own perspective, we look beyond the functional, pragmatic brief. Our job is to make the brief sing, creating architecture that says something about our culture and the civilisation we live in. In Northumberland, for example, we took inspiration from the cutting tools essential to the mining industry – creating something beautiful out of the mechanical. Something hopeful out of the despair caused by the decline in the mining industry. At Shenzhen University, we've taken the Chinese mantra of unity and modernity and fused it with the undulating lines of the surrounding hillsides to create a building that flows toward a dynamic future – for the country and the students that will forge it.

Architecture has the same language as music. It's a rhythmic aesthetic in which every duff note detracts from the harmony of the whole piece. That's why we focus on the process of architecture, rather than the product. The place, the site, the rooms, the machines and systems, the design. And, almost more important than any of those, the dreams. In this way, we create a rich diversity of work. Individual solutions for individual locations. You should never be able to uproot a building from its location and transplant it into another. A beautiful building in the wrong location becomes not only an ugly building but an offensive building, culturally, geographically, politically, historically and socially.

It all comes back to the human dimension. A dimension that curiously comes some way down the list of priorities for some. Not here. RMJM has practised social architecture since its formation. RM and JM would have it no other way: "the right design in the right place in the right time at the right price" as Stirrat's favourite saying went. We believe in a human modernism that matches simplicity and function with intrigue and understanding.

Of course, good architecture needs good clients as much as good architects. We need our clients to have ambition. Although we like a coherent brief, we encourage our clients to imagine a better way. Most of all, we need them to understand the need for questions. Because without questions, you get no answers. We do, however, live in the real world – which means we are fully aware of the commercial imperatives of any project. Our holistic approach to architecture doesn't stop at the drawing board. We want to deliver our designs. Only then can there be consistency in vision and consistency in realisation.

The beauty of our belief in process over product is its transference value. Each design director within each RMJM office has his or her own working process – which is why there is no such thing as a signature RMJM building – but our design community does share a common vision. And whether we're masterplanning a whole new city or designing a simple box for living, we imbue that process with passion. Always passion.

DREAMS

A BUILDING WITHOUT A DREAM
IS A BUILDING. A BUILDING WITH
A DREAM IS ARCHITECTURE.
GOOD ARCHITECTURE REQUIRES
A CLEAR CONCEPTUAL ASPIRATION
AND AMBITION. ARCHITECTURE,
DIFFERENT FROM MERE BUILDING,
MUST APPEAL NOT ONLY TO OUR
SENSES BUT ALSO TO OUR
INTELLECT.

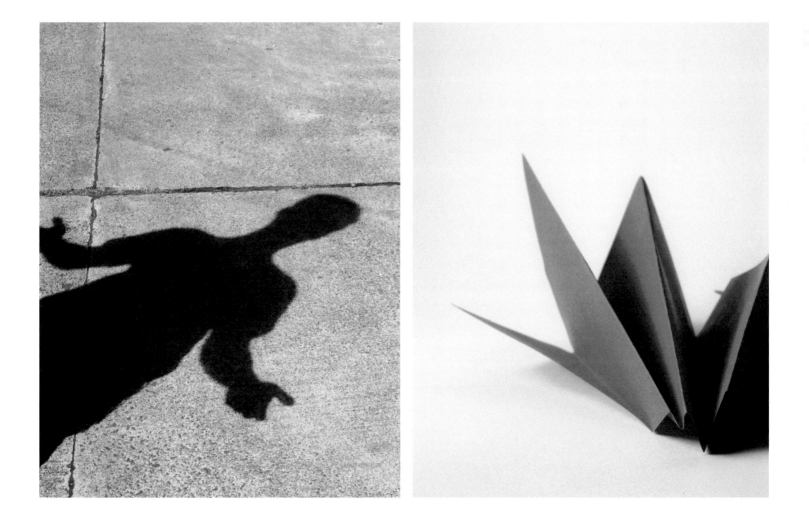

CONCEPTUAL ASPIRATIONS

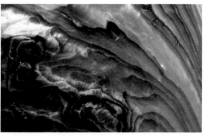

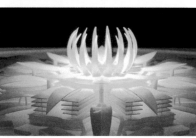

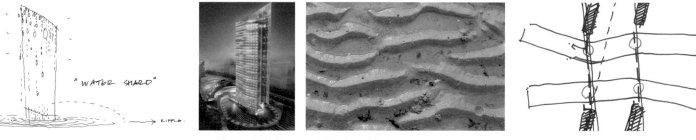

"WATER SHARD"

RIPPLE

PLACE

WORKING WITH DIVERSE CLIENTS
ON SMALL AND LARGE PROJECTS,
WITHIN DIFFERENT COUNTRIES
AND CULTURES ACROSS THE
WORLD, RMJM HAS LEARNED
TO BE SENSITIVE, TO CARE AND
ENJOY THE PLACES IN WHICH
WE WORK AND TO CELEBRATE
THROUGH OUR DESIGN THE
UNIQUE QUALITIES OF EACH
AND EVERY CONTEXT.

FORM AND SPACE

SOCIAL AND POLITICAL

CULTURE AND CHARACTER
THE MORE TIME SPENT UNDERSTANDING A
LOCAL CULTURE AND ITS ASPIRATIONS, THE MORE
REWARDING AND MEANINGFUL OUR ARCHITECTURE
WILL BE TO THAT COMMUNITY.

**WOODHORN: NORTHUMBERLAND MUSEUM,
ARCHIVES AND COUNTRY PARK, ASHINGTON, UK**

Woodhorn is a brave new building type in the North-east town
of Ashington housing a mining museum, gallery and county
record archive facility. Situated in the QEII Country Park,
the flagship visitor attraction will provide information on
Northumberland's social and cultural history, from its coal
mining heritage to community and family history. The serrated
teeth of coal cutting machinery inspired the dramatic roof
form of the building, representing the danger and energy of
the coal industry – previously the lifeblood of the area – while
creating a contemporary statement for future.

TOP RIGHT
Inspiration for the roof's
serrated form was found
in coal cutting machinery
used in the past.

RIGHT AND FAR RIGHT
Archive photographs
of Woodhorn Colliery.

FACING PAGE TOP
A visualisation showing
how the new building
sits on the site with the
existing listed buildings,
which have also been
sensitively restored.

FACING PAGE BOTTOM
An aerial photograph
and visualisation show
how the low-lying
building sits in the
scenic QEII Country Park.

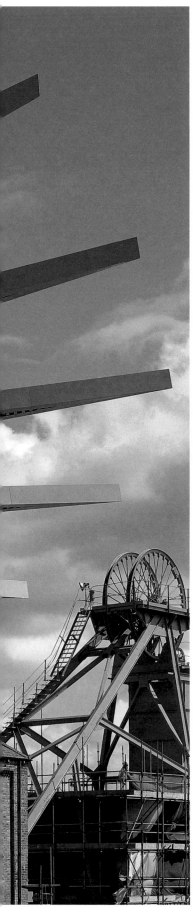

FACING PAGE
The new building in
its historical context.

TOP
The roof form of the new
structure contributes to
the dramatic skyline of
the site.

BOTTOM
A deliberate decision
was taken not to use the
external materials of the
existing buildings to clad
the new building. Instead,
complementary materials
were chosen to define
the new element in
consultation with both
the Northumberland
County Council
conservation officer
and English Heritage.
Materials used include
gabion walls (filled with
locally sourced crushed
rock), curtain walling,
galvanised metal and
burnt orange render.

FORM AND SPACE
OUR ROLE IN URBAN DESIGN INITIATIVES IS
COMPARABLE TO THAT OF A GARDENER — SOWING
SEEDS OF OPPORTUNITY FOR FUTURE GENERATIONS
TO WORK WITH, DEVELOPING PHYSICAL FORMS AND
STRUCTURES TO SUPPORT THE COMPLEX MIX OF
SOCIAL, ENVIRONMENTAL AND ECONOMIC FORCES
THAT SUSTAIN OUR LIVING CITIES. LIGHT, SPACE,
PROPORTION, GEOMETRY AND DENSITY ARE THE
MEANS AND DISCIPLINES WITH WHICH WE WORK
TO FASHION THESE PLACES. AND RUNNING RIGHT
THROUGH THE CORE OF THESE IS AN UNDERSTANDING
THAT THESE PLACES ARE FOR PEOPLE.

CUSTOM HOUSE QUAY, GLASGOW, UK

Visualisation of the
Clydeside boardwalk.

Custom House Quay, which forms Glasgow city centre's main
frontage to the River Clyde, currently lies abandoned, a
desolate strip of former industrial land. However, an ongoing
urban renaissance is helping to connect the city back to its
river. RMJM's proposal seeks to maximise the potential of this
site and create a prime location and public space, and an
opportunity to give Glasgow a bold new international
waterfront image. Central to this urban design project is the
creation of a series of public 'river rooms' and spaces which
are linked to the city's wider linear park plan, a park that will
eventually link various riverside communities running east to
west along the River Clyde.

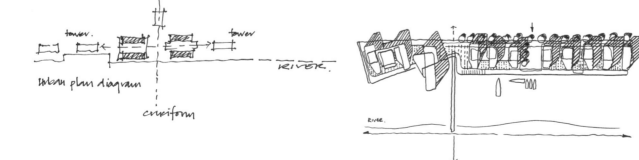

urban plan diagram

cruciform

tower.

tower

RIVER.

RIVER.

TOP
Visualisations of the new streetscapes including Cathedral Square.

MIDDLE
Visualisation of the aerial night view.

BOTTOM
Sketches showing the urban 'river rooms'.

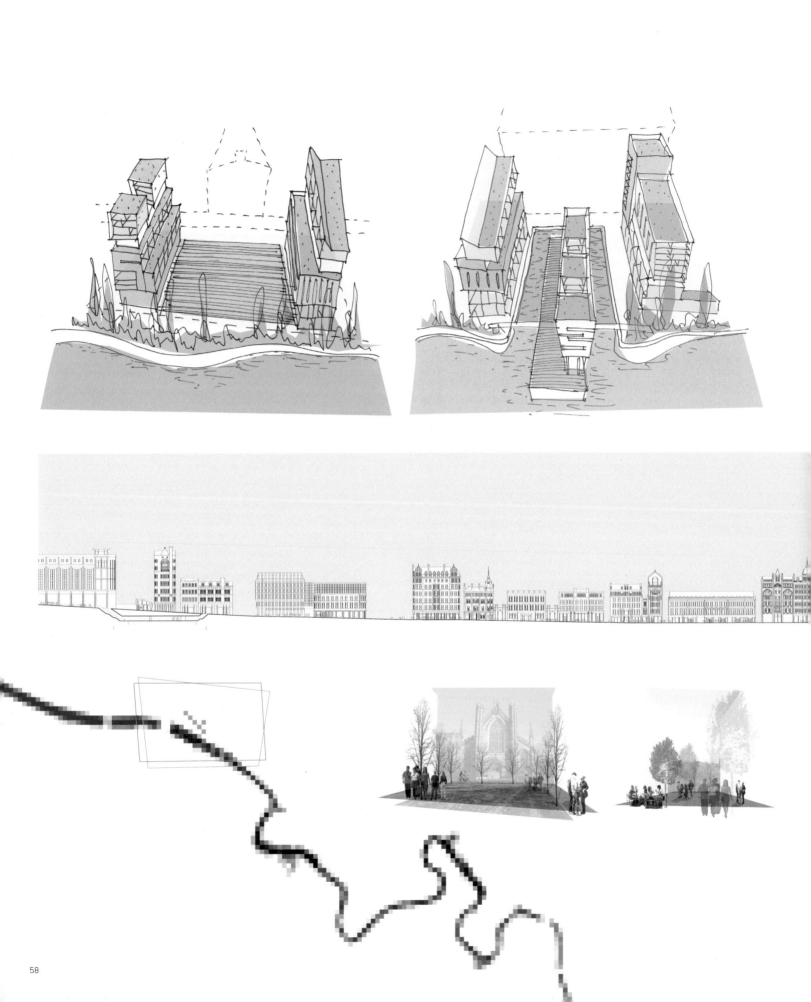

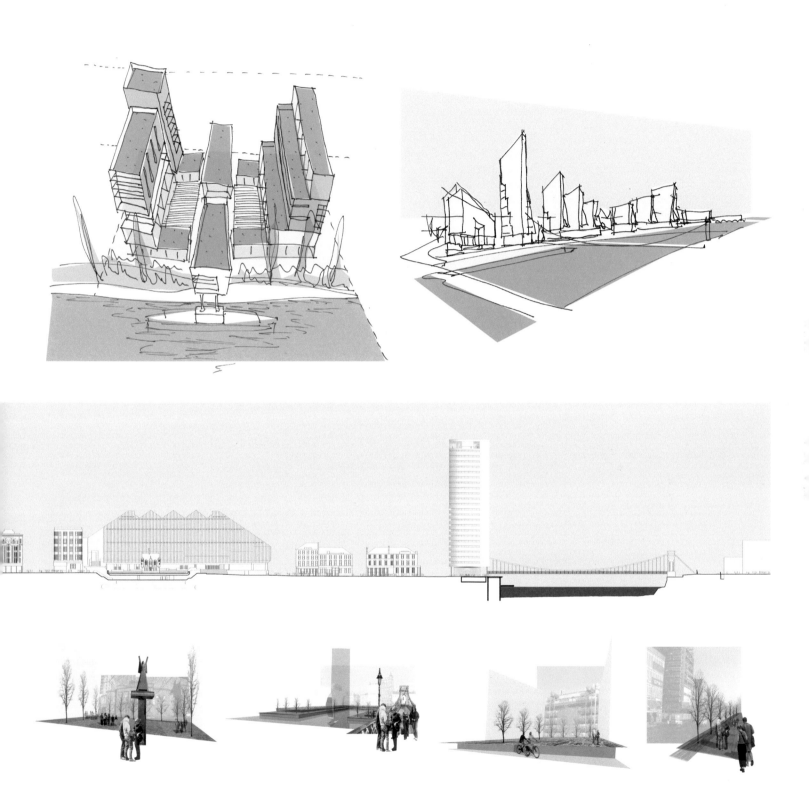

TOP
Sketches showing the
development of the
public spaces along
the quayside.

MIDDLE
Elevation of Buchanan
Street with the river
and new quayside at
its southernmost tip.

BOTTOM
The River Clyde and
its new 'river rooms'.

MORPHOLOGY
THE UNDERSTANDING OF THE TYPOLOGY OF BUILDINGS
AND, MOST IMPORTANTLY, THE SPACES BETWEEN THEM
IS AT THE CORE OF ALL URBAN DESIGN STUDY WITHIN
AND AROUND OUR CITIES.

LEITH DOCKS DEVELOPMENT FRAMEWORK, EDINBURGH, UK

In creating the underlying framework for the future sustained
evolution of Leith, RMJM's challenge was to provide the basis
for a seamless integration of the old and the new on this 170
hectare waterfront site. Acting as a catalyst for the creation
of a mixed, balanced and inclusive community, integrating
the strong local identity of Leith, RMJM's proposals provide
design quality, spatial structure and a public realm strategy
befitting Scotland's capital city.

NO
DOG
FOULING

TYPOLOGY
WE HAVE A FASCINATION WITH ARCHITECTURAL
TYPOLOGIES. LIKE ARCHAEOLOGISTS EXPLORING
A DIG, WE ENJOY TRYING TO BOTH PRESCRIBE
AND INTERPRET THE NUANCES, CODES AND HIDDEN
MEANINGS THAT ARE EMBODIED IN ARCHITECTURAL
PLAN FORMS.

RESIDENTIAL PLANS

Housebuilders call their residential types 'product' and estate
agents call it 'home'. At RMJM, we call our plan diagrams 'living
spaces'. As designers we study the intimate arrangement of
space within our residential developments, opening spaces
up to present more dynamic and alternative patterns of living.
Large numbers of residential developers resort to formulaic
and staid pattern book designs. Sometimes very simple
changes to these plans can have a huge and positive influence
on our daily private rituals.

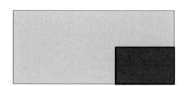

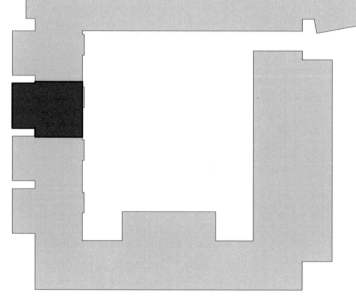

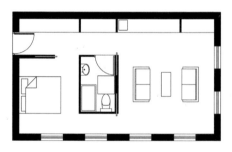

TOP AND BOTTOM LEFT
Townhouse – Plan for
an intimate courtyard
development.

TOP AND BOTTOM RIGHT
Studio – High-rise
and high density studio
housing type for
inner city.

**FACING PAGE
TOP**
Mews House – Single
aspect linear mews
house plan.

MIDDLE LEFT
Apartment –
Contemporary and
compact retirement
apartments for the
over 50s.

MIDDLE RIGHT
Terrace House –
Simple terrace type
repeated to create
street frontage.

BOTTOM
Flatted – High-rise
riverside residential
accommodation.

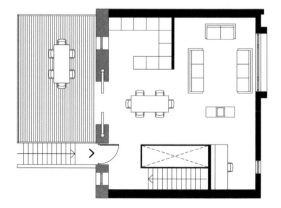

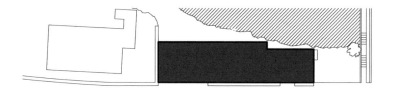

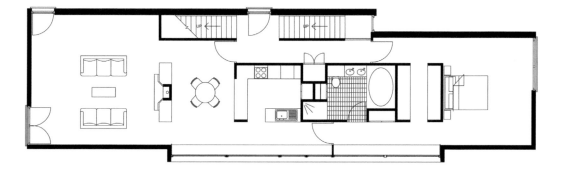

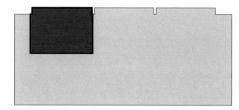

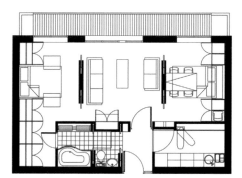

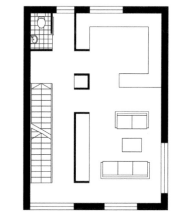

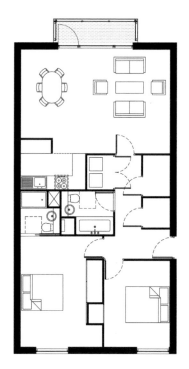

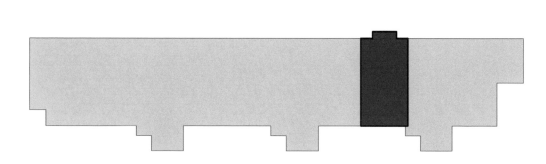

TYPOLOGY

CONVENTION CENTRES

The mammoth proportions and simple plans of exhibition halls need not equate to unimaginative design. In recent years, RMJM has developed an expertise in the creation of world-class convention spaces capable of hosting the most prestigious of international events. In Beijing for the 2008 Olympic Games, in Dubai for the World Bank and IMF annual meetings and in one of India's largest cities, the rapidly expanding Kolkata, RMJM creates light, bright, fully flexible and functional spaces that inspire and lift the spirits.

TOP
Visualisations showing
the pagoda-inspired
front elevation, aerial
view, landscaping and
auditorium.

BOTTOM
Construction underway
in Beijing of the
270,000m² Olympic
Green Convention
Centre emerging on
the 12.2 hectare site.

65

The Kolkata International Convention Centre, one of the largest planned mixed-use developments in India, will cater for international exhibitions and conventions of up to 2,000 delegates.

The new Abu Dhabi National Exhibition Centre is a 55,000m² multi-purpose complex containing exhibition space, ancillary accommodation and pedestrian square.

CLIMATE
LOCAL CLIMATE AND GEOGRAPHY FUNDAMENTALLY
INFLUENCE OUR ARCHITECTURE; ENTIRE CULTURES
ARE IMBUED WITH CHARACTERISTICS THAT ARE A
RESULT OF GEOGRAPHY AND LOCATION.

DESIGNING FOR THE GREAT BRITISH WEATHER

RMJM explores different architectural forms and building
envelopes in order to achieve an environmentally appropriate
architecture that is clear, conceptual and contextual –
architecture appropriate to both our climate and our culture.
Our site-specific designs respond in imaginative and inclusive
ways. In the UK, our residential projects are obviously designed
to keep the rain out and the heat in but we also need
buildings which are not wholly introverted, conservative and
private but which are celebratory and inspiring.

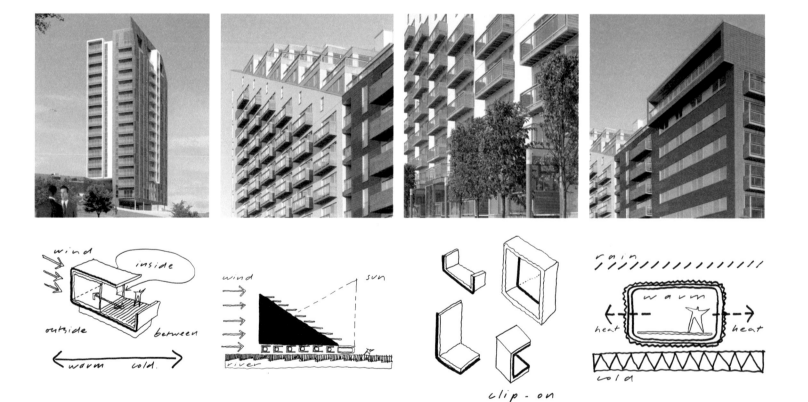

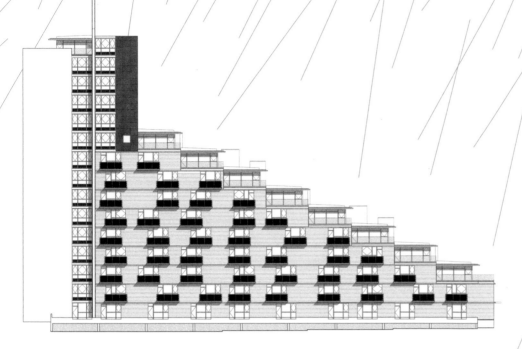

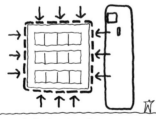

warm

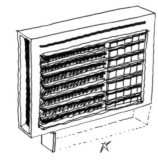

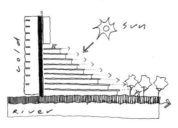

cold sun

river

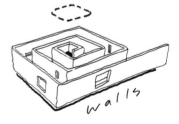

walls

A selection of projects were specifically designed with the great British weather in mind: Dundas Wharf, Glasgow Harbour, Homes for the Future and Festival Park. They illustrate the meteorological mindset, utilising environmental shield, sun terraces, balconies, wrapped space, super-insulation, windbreakers, south and north aspects and protective walls.

Each of the 155 apartments at Glasgow Harbour has a private balcony or terrace, sheltered from the wind and making the most of the sun.

SOCIAL AND POLITICAL
ARCHITECTURE IS OFTEN MOTIVATED BY TRANSIENT
ECONOMIC, SOCIAL OR POLITICAL IDEALS. WE SHOULD
RESPOND TO THESE WITH ARTISTIC AMBITION, HUMAN
UNDERSTANDING AND PASSION.

**SIGHTHILL COMMUNITY ONE STOP SHOP,
GLASGOW, UK**

Plagued by violence, drugs and health-related issues,
Sighthill has a population of 7,500 and ranks as one of the
five most economically deprived and socially excluded
communities in Scotland. Unemployment is three times the
Scottish national average and heart disease rates are 120
per cent above the Scottish national average. It is Scotland's
most ethnically diverse, multi-cultural community with a
Black and Minority Ethnic population 638 per cent above
average. This new community facility will offer gateway
advice and support to residents on housing, asylum, credit
union, tenants' association, mental health, healthy eating,
employment and training.

FACING PAGE
The derelict supermarket
which will house SCOSS.

TOP
A selection of elevation
studies exploring the use
of colour.

BOTTOM
A visualisation of the
refurbished premises.
The SCOSS committee
wholeheartedly
embraces the new
colourful skin.

73

NO SITE IS EVER THE SAME.

ORIENTATION   TOPOGRAPHY

SITE

SITE SPECIFIC QUALITIES
DO WE BENEFIT FROM A SOUTH ASPECT OR FROM A PARTICULAR VIEW? ARE THERE REMARKABLE SITE FEATURES THAT WE CAN FRAME THROUGH A DOORWAY OR WINDOW? WHICH WAY DO THE PREVAILING WINDS BLOW AND WHICH TREE SPECIES WOULD THE SITE SUPPORT?

THESE ARE QUESTIONS AND THOUGHTS WE MIGHT ASK OF OURSELVES AS WE BEGIN TO FORMULATE THE CONTEXTUAL AND ARCHITECTURAL RESPONSES IN OUR DESIGN.

BRIGHTON TOWER, BRIGHTON, UK

"The Central Seafront node provides a distinct opportunity for tall buildings. The location of this area in the heart of the cultural, retail and commercial core of the city suggests the possibility of some high quality tall buildings."
(Extract from Brighton and Hove Local Authority tall buildings study and supplementary planning guidance.)

"Tall buildings can enhance skylines, particularly if their tops are designed with flair – perhaps thrillingly slender or strikingly patterned. They mark the centre of a city and provide a point of orientation which is visible from far away."
(The Civic Trust 2001)

Many of the high-rise development proposals across the UK today are not supported by a local authority tall buildings study or an appropriate planning framework. Brighton and Hove Council has, however, been proactive in preparing a comprehensive supplementary planning guide for high-rise designs which has been an essential reference for RMJM in the development of an outline tower design for Brighton waterfront.

The design challenge for RMJM was to satisfy and excite all parties at both an intellectual and simple subjective level. The objective was for the local planning authority and the wider public to embrace the building positively, both critically and emotionally. The building's form, its proportion, geometry and structure, is visually intelligent and underpinned by sound decision-making and artistic integrity, and most importantly its dramatic site-specific relationship.

The Slice: *Chain Pier, Brighton* by John Constable with new addition by RMJM.

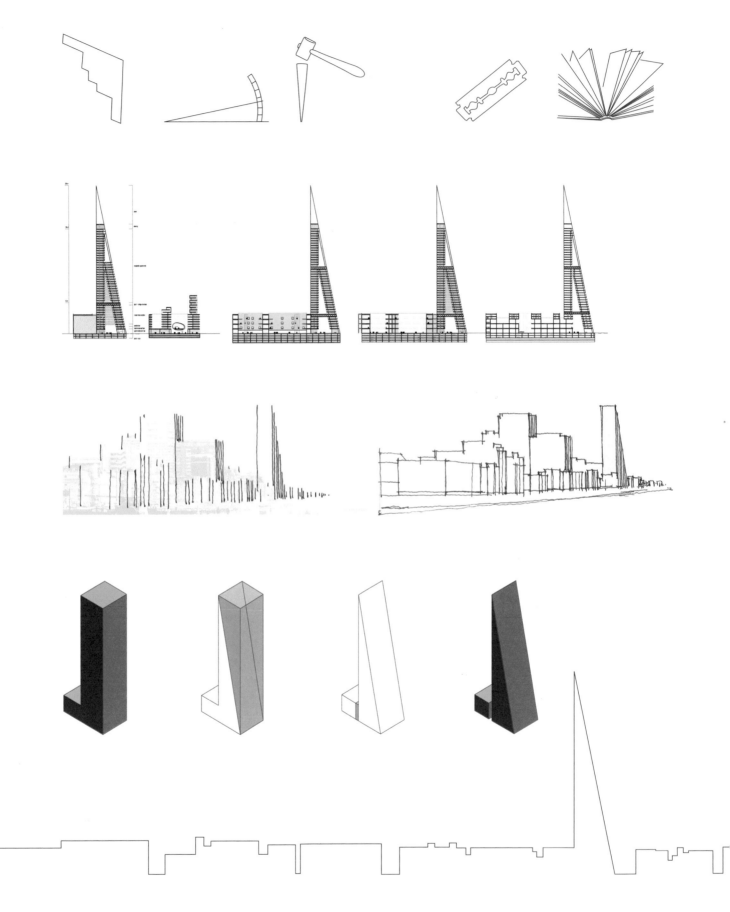

TOP
Inspirational diagonals
included scissors, origami,
stealth bombers and
high heels.

SECOND ROW
Sections exploring the
mix of uses in the tower.

THIRD ROW
Diagrammatical studies
of the building's form and
its impact on the skyline.

FOURTH ROW
Elevation studies.

BOTTOM
The new structure sitting
on the Brighton skyline.

ASPECT
IMAGINE THE VIEW OR IMPRESSION SOMEONE
MIGHT HAVE WHEN THEY ARE WITHIN A BUILDING
AND LOOKING OUT. IS THERE A SOUTH ASPECT
OR A REMARKABLE SITE FEATURE THAT CAN BE
FRAMED THROUGH A DOORWAY OR WINDOW?
CAN WE POSITIVELY RELATE OUR INTERNAL
ARCHITECTURE TO OUR UNIQUE SITE FEATURES
AND CLIMATE? DO WE UNDERSTAND OUR ASPECT?

**COMMONWEALTH GAMES MASTERPLAN, GLASGOW
SYETUN RESIDENTIAL DEVELOPMENT, MOSCOW**

In Moscow and in Scotland, both projects focus on the
waterfront aspect of the buildings. The masterplan for the
Commonwealth Games village, which forms part of Glasgow's
bid for the 2014 Games, radiates from the centre and the
river. A series of districts or communities address the open
space to the east and the existing fabric to the west.
In Moscow, the focus of the scheme is to create positive
outdoor space with degrees of privacy from private to
semi-public to public shared gardens, all leading to a
tranquil lake on the north edge of the site.

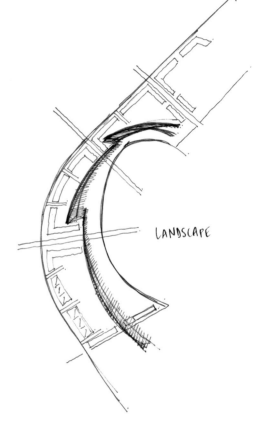

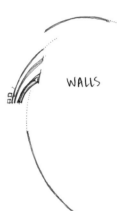

WALLS

WATER

LANDSCAPE

TOP
Conceptual development
of project with an
emphasis on the
different layers all
relating back to the
River Clyde.

BOTTOM
Maximising the views
of Victory Park and the
nearby lake in Moscow.

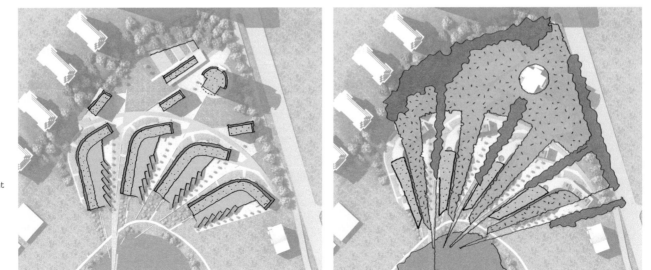

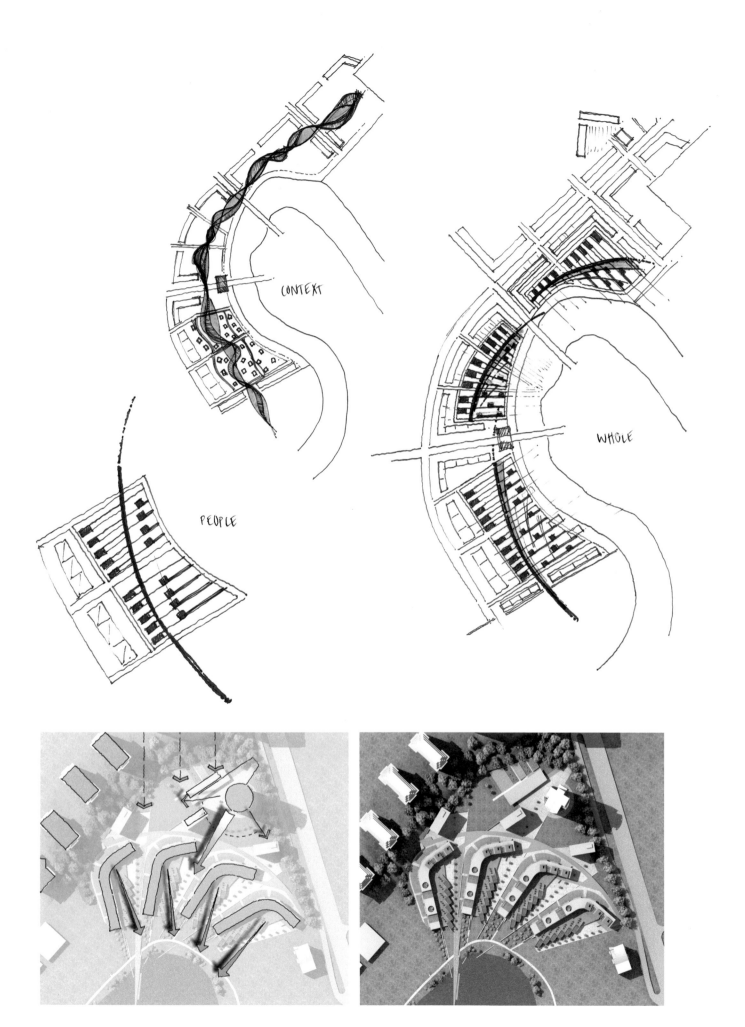

CONTEXT

PEOPLE

WHOLE

ORIENTATION
A COMPASS READING, A DIRECTION, A COURSE,
A POINT OF REFERENCE. HOW DOES OUR
ARCHITECTURE RELATE TO ITS CONTEXT? MAKING
POSITIVE AND CLEAR DECISIONS ABOUT A BUILDING'S
ORIENTATION RELATIVE TO ITS SITING IS ESSENTIAL.

NORTH GLASGOW COLLEGE, UK

The North Glasgow College campus responds to a direct
north/south axial alignment. The building, like a compass,
is directional and wholly appropriate as it aims to inspire
confidence for people bettering themselves through
education. The building and landscape design celebrates the
'happy coincidence' of two different grids – the city grid and
the ordnance grid – by introducing a diagonal 'cut' into the
urban block. The area that is effectively cut away forms a new
public space. This new space is orientated in a south-westerly
direction to maximise midday and afternoon sun and provide
a much needed civic space for a neglected community.

TOP
The building form
explained – a simple
rectangle with a
cut-out wedge.

BOTTOM
Archive images of
Springburn where
the college is located.

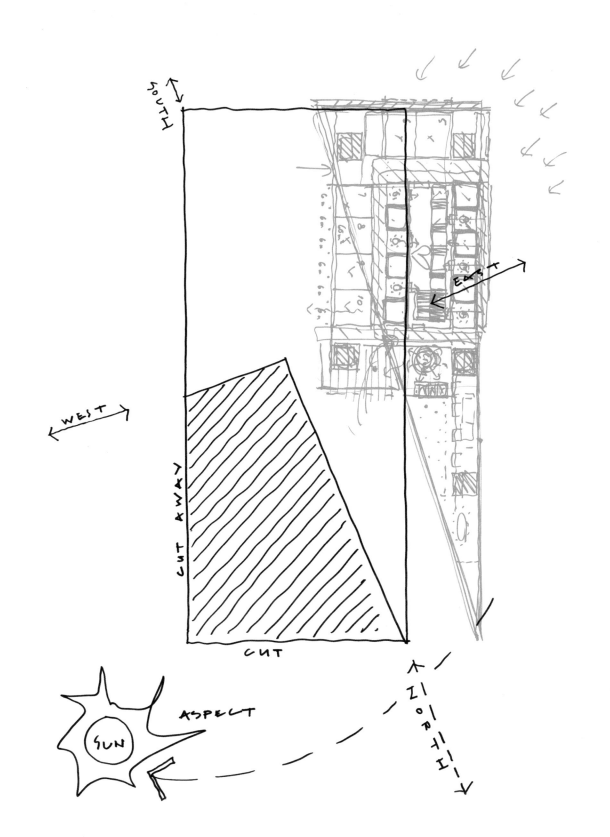

SOUTH

WEST

EAST

CUT AWAY

CUT

SUN

ASPECT

NORTH

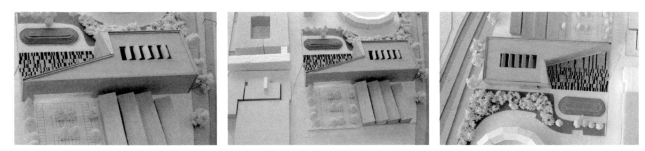

TOP
A sketch from one of the
first project meetings.

BOTTOM
Model studies of
the new building
in its setting.

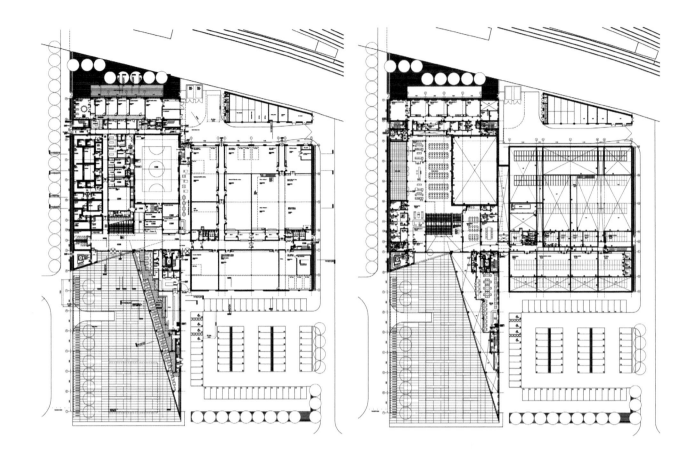

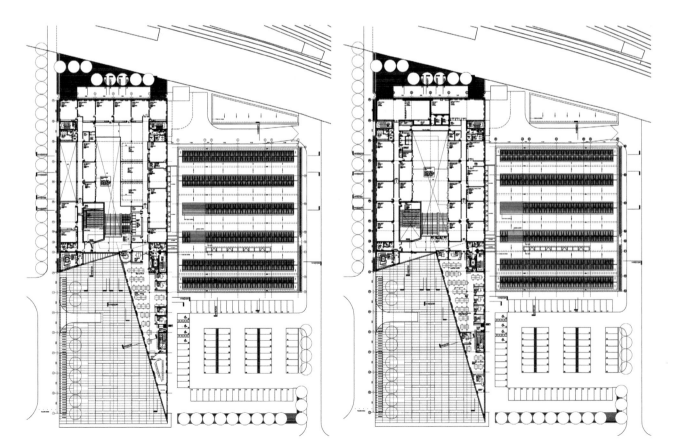

Four of the six floor-
plans: ground, first,
second and third.

TOP
Final visualisation.

MIDDLE AND BOTTOM
Elevation studies using
a variety of materials
and internal studies.

VIEWS AND VISTAS

THE CONSIDERED VIEWS AND VISTAS WITHIN
OUR CITIES AND LANDSCAPES ARE THE DYNAMIC
INGREDIENTS THAT DIFFERENTIATE AND IDENTIFY
A PLACE. CONSIDER THE FRAMED VIEW OF PARIS'
EIFFEL TOWER, THE TREES IN NEW YORK'S CENTRAL
PARK, THE QUIET GEORGIAN ARCHITECTURE OF AN
EDINBURGH STREET OR THE PEAK IN HONG KONG:
ALL CITIES WHICH, REGARDLESS OF THEIR SCALE,
HAVE DISTINCTIVE LOCAL FEATURES THAT DESERVE
TO BE CELEBRATED.

PRINCES DOCK, LIVERPOOL , UK

Liverpool has always been a city defined by the views to and
from the waterfront and any intervention at Princes Dock
needs to be carefully modelled to respect these prominent
views to landmarks such as the Three Graces. The proposed
development has a strong vertical element and, therefore, the
challenge for the design team was to use this verticality as
a positive feature adding to the cluster of high-rise
developments on this key gateway site into the city.

RIGHT
The tower will be
articulated by shifting
elements both vertically
and horizontally at key
points, modifying to the
mass and facade detail.
This has the benefit of
allowing the architecture
to respond to the
heights of key buildings
around the development,
strengthening its
integration into the
existing urban fabric.
The multi-layering
creates different views
of the tower as you
move around it.

FACING PAGE
The climatic conditions
were key drivers in the
development of the
design, in particular the
form of the tower, as
the design seeks to
maximise the best views
with minimum solar
exposure; at the same
time limiting the extent
of the shadow that will
be cast by the new
building.

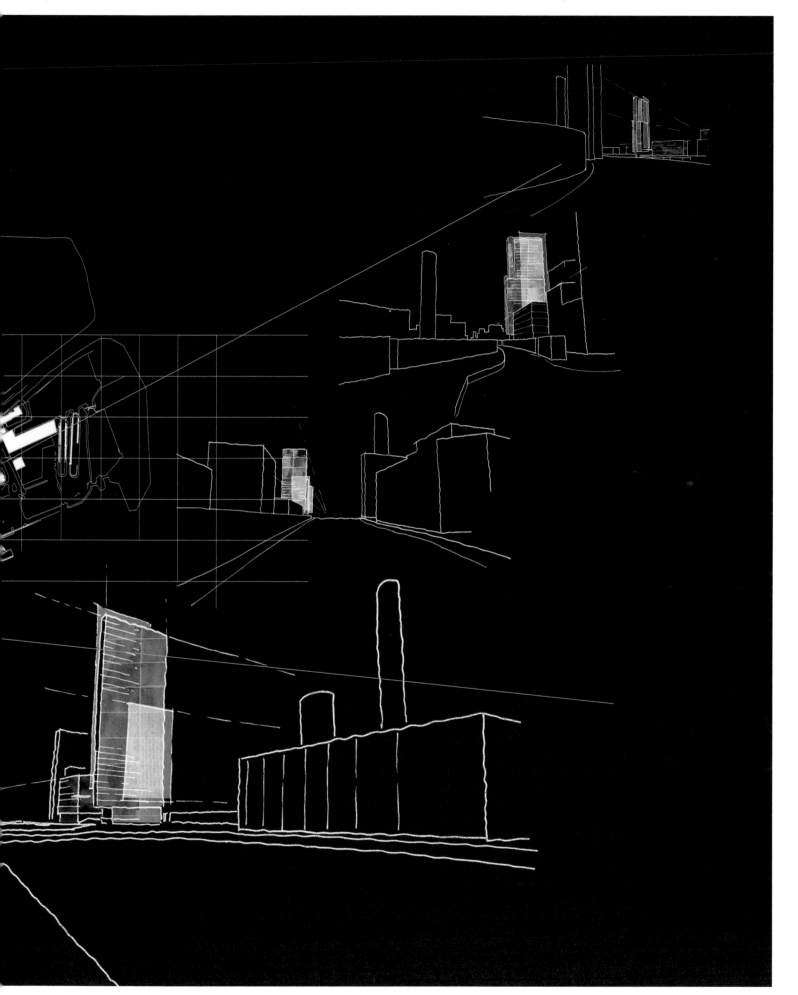

RMJM was commissioned to produce a number of concept proposals for a seven star hotel in the heart of Beijing. Drawing on traditional ancient Chinese architecture, the Pagoda form in particular, the proposals reflect the new international and modern Beijing.

TOP LEFT
The 25-storey tower development at Swiss Cottage in London will accommodate offices, residential and retail uses.

TOP RIGHT
The 80-storey Dubai Tower in Qatar will rise 400 metres above the Arabian Gulf.

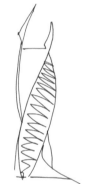

TOP LEFT
The Kiss by Auguste Rodin inspired the thinking behind the City Palace Tower in Moscow. Sketch development shows the sensual beginnings behind the Tower's form.

TOP RIGHT AND FACING PAGE
The organic form of the building, reminiscent of the twisting domes of St Basils on Red Square, is made of two metaphorical parts – male and female – which intertwine as they rise up the building.

Designed in collaboration with Scottish artist Karen Forbes, the project mixes passion and drama with a conventional square footprint ideal for offices and other commercial uses.

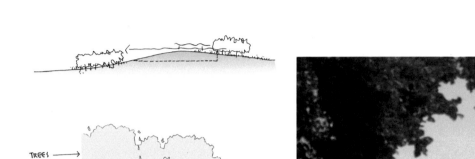

TOPOGRAPHY
THE SCENERY, THE LANDSCAPE AND THE GEOGRAPHY
OF EVERY SITE, WHEREVER WE ARE IN THE WORLD,
ARE FUNDAMENTALLY DIFFERENT AND, THEREFORE,
DEMAND A DIFFERENT ARCHITECTURAL AND
CONTEXTUAL RESPONSE.

KENT HISTORY CENTRE , UK

RMJM's competition response for the Kent History Centre
took inspiration from the natural topography of the site –
the landscaped grounds of Leeds Castle. The RMJM team
provided a pragmatic response to the functional needs of
the brief, reconciling it with the sensitivities of building on
a historic site. By placing the archive material below ground
the repositories were contained within a secure, stable
environment and their visual impact minimised in relation
to key views from the site.

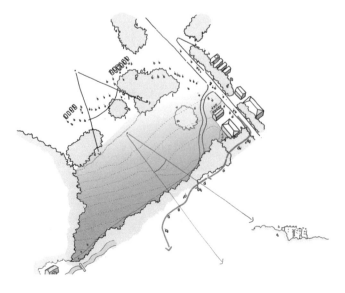

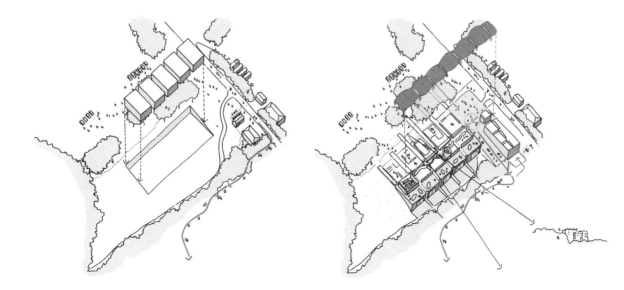

CLOCKWISE FROM
TOP LEFT
Initial sketches exploring
the site's topography;
The roof of the low-lying
pavilion was designed to
float over the glass
enclosure, its organic
form responding to the
linear nature of the
surrounding landscape;
Sketches of the site
exploring the views,
massing and routes;
Interior sketch of
an archive hall.

LANDSCAPE
THE SETTING, BACKDROP, PANORAMA, TERRAIN, VIEW, SCENERY, GREENERY, ENVIRONMENT OF A PLACE.

THE SCOTTISH PARLIAMENT, EDINBURGH, UK

The evocative words "the Parliament sits in the land" were prominent on EMBT/RMJM's original competition-winning submission. These few words eloquently summarise the fundamental philosophical relationship of the Parliament and its designed landscape to the wider 'natural' landscape beyond and to Scotland itself. They are intrinsically linked and inseparable. The inseparability of building and land dissolves all the conventional architectural rules no more so than when grass slopes become grass roofs and benches are raised up off the ground.

The role of the landscape, itself a substantial construction project, was fundamental in the realisation of the concept of the Scottish Parliament sitting "in the land" and is faithful to the initial concept design. The symbiosis is completed by the planting of Sticky Catch Fly, indigenous to the Crags, in the open joints of the gabions.

THE LANDSCAPE BUILDING
A BUILDING AS A LANDSCAPE IS DIFFERENT FROM A
BUILDING WITHIN A LANDSCAPE. THE FORMER SEEKS TO
HARMONISE AND INTEGRATE WITH THE LAND AND THE
LATTER DETERMINES A MORE FORMAL AND CLASSICAL
OBJECT STATUS RELATIVE TO ITS SURROUNDINGS.

A PRACTICE PREOCCUPATION

RMJM has a long tradition of landscape buildings, buildings
that are fundamentally conceived as having a direct
relationship with the landscape. The practice has a clear
commitment to and interest in a human and democratic
architecture that is open and accessible. From the practice's
early post war public buildings through to our collaborative
work on the Scottish Parliament, the practice has
demonstrated an intellectual engagement with buildings that
are rooted in specific landscapes. Exemplar buildings are the
Commonwealth Pool, the practice's work at Stirling University
and at York University, and more recently the William Gates
building at Cambridge University. More figurative design is
evident in the Falkirk Wheel Visitor Centre where the buildings
integrate with the park landscape to offset the dramatic
structure of the boat lift and elevated aqueduct.

CLOCKWISE FROM
TOP LEFT
Glasgow Nautical College;
The William Gates Building
at the University of
Cambridge;
The Scottish Public
Pensions Agency in
Galashiels;
The Lifestyle Academy
at Newcastle College;
The Falkirk Wheel
and Visitor Centre;
Glaxo Wellcome World HQ;
The University of
Hertfordshire; The Royal
Commonwealth Pool,
Edinburgh.

CONNECTIVITY

THE EXTENT TO WHICH A PLACE OR BUILDING
IS PERMEABLE AND ACCESSIBLE DEPENDS ON
HOW WELL IT FORGES LINKS, MAKES CONNECTIONS
AND OVERCOMES BARRIERS AND IMPEDIMENTS. A
PRINCIPAL CHALLENGE IN THE DESIGN OF A BUILDING
OR DYNAMIC URBAN SPACE IS TO RESOLVE AND
POSITIVELY MANAGE CONNECTIONS AND SEPARATIONS
BETWEEN WIDELY DIFFERENT ACTIVITIES.

SHENZHEN UNIVERSITY TOWN LIBRARY AND ADMINISTRATIVE CENTRE, CHINA

The long, undulating form of RMJM's library and administrative
centre in Shenzhen, China, echoes the gentle form of the
surrounding hills. Forming the gateway to a new tripartite
university campus, the pedestrian bridge will connect two of
the campus' principal areas. The administrative centre is at the
head of the scheme and functions as the administrative nucleus
for the three universities; the central library acts as the 'spine'
from which the three universities connect and function.

TOP
Visualisation illustrating
the linking of two
campuses and a site
photograph from
April 2006.

BOTTOM AND
FACING PAGE TOP
Night-time visualisation
and model study show
the undulating form of
the building.

FACING PAGE
BOTTOM
Masterplan.

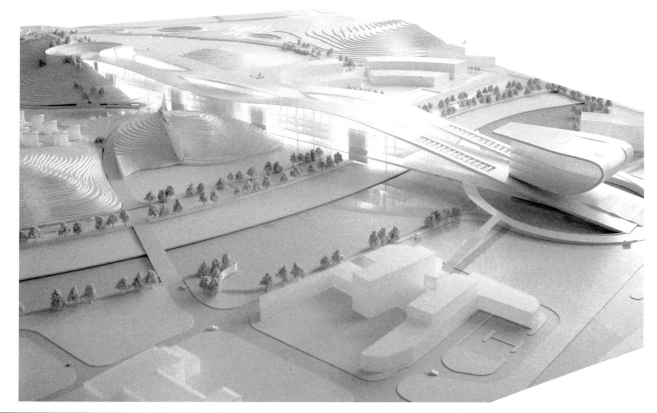

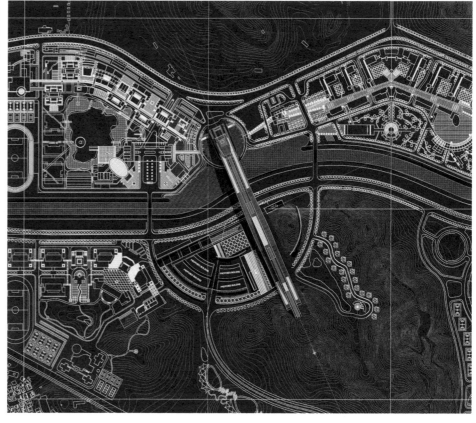

ROOMS
THE ORDERING OF ROOMS AND THE HIERARCHY OF SPATIAL RELATIONSHIPS BETWEEN INTERNAL AND EXTERNAL SPACES OF A BUILDING COMPLEX ARE CRITICAL. FOR A BUILDING TO FUNCTION WELL WE HAVE TO CAREFULLY CONSIDER HOW FUTURE ACTIVITIES WILL BE SUPPORTED. THE BALANCING OF PRESCRIPTIVE DESIGN SOLUTIONS AND FLEXIBLE OPEN SPACE PROVISION IS A CENTRAL DESIGN CHALLENGE ON ALL PROJECTS.

ORGANISATION

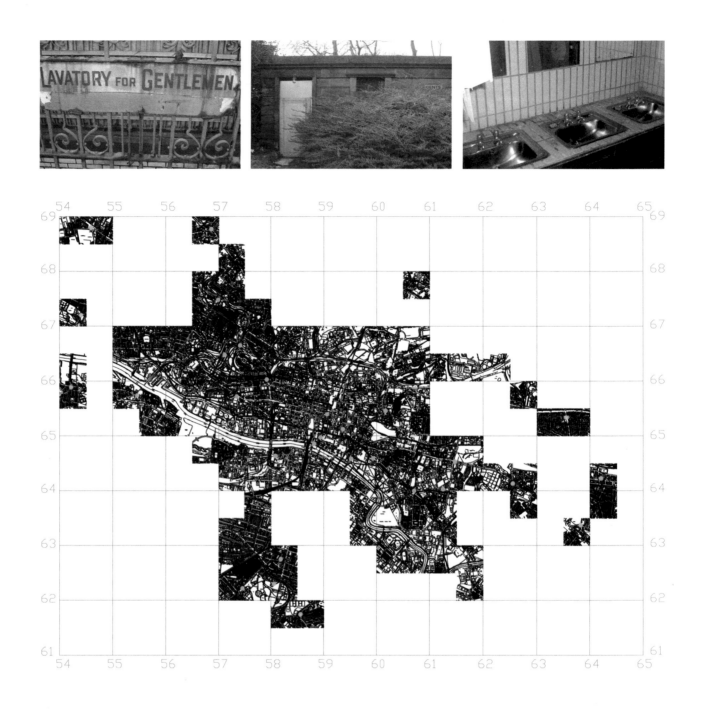

SIMPLE BUILDINGS
WHETHER VERY LARGE OR VERY SMALL, SIMPLE
BUILDINGS ARE NOT AN OUTCOME OF SCALE BUT
RATHER SPACE. LARGE BUILDINGS LIKE STADIUMS
CAN BE SPATIALLY SIMPLE, ONE BIG ROOM OR
VOLUME. SIMPLE BUILDINGS CAN BE SMALL, TOO,
LIKE A TOILET BLOCK FOR EXAMPLE.

PUBLIC UTILITIES

Many cities across the world have a network of public toilets,
historically woven into their urban fabric. Today, many of these
toilets lie disused, sharing a relationship by being of the same
type and set at strategic points. Due to their unique
characteristics, an opportunity exists to revitalise this lost
space, providing elements that improve, enhance and enliven
life in the city.

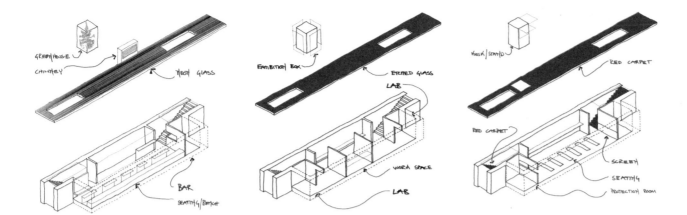

GREENHOUSE
CHIMNEY
NEON GLASS
BAR
SEATING/BENCH

EXHIBITION BOX
ETCHED GLASS
LAB
WORK SPACE
LAB

KIOSK/STAND
RED CARPET
RED CARPET
SCREEN
SEATING
PROJECTION ROOM

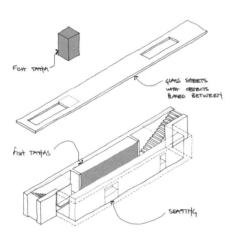

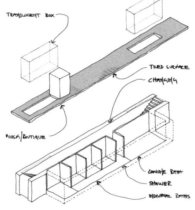

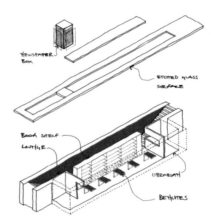

FISH TANK
GLASS SHEETS WITH OBJECTS PLACED BETWEEN
FISH TANKS
SEATING

TRANSLUCENT BOX
TILED SURFACE
CHANGING
KIOSK/BOUTIQUE
COMMUNAL BATH
SHOWER
INDIVIDUAL BATHS

NEWSPAPER BOX
ETCHED GLASS SURFACE
BOOK SHELF
LOUNGE
LIBRARIAN
BENCHES

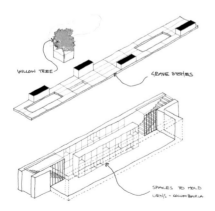

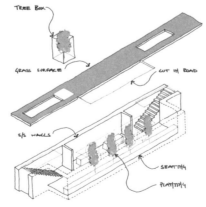

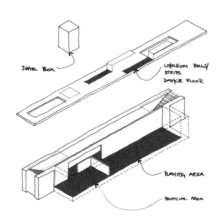

WILLOW TREE
GRAVE STONES
SPACES TO HOLD URNS - COLUMBARIA

TREE BOX
GRASS SURFACE
CUT IN ROAD
E/S WALLS
SEATING
PLANTING

JUKE BOX
LINOLEUM ROLLS/ STRIPS
DANCE FLOOR
PLANTING AREA
ACOUSTICAL AREA

FACING PAGE
Glasgow has in the region of 30 unused public utility buildings.

TOP TO BOTTOM, LEFT TO RIGHT
Sketch studies for proposed new uses: Coffee shop; Darkrooms; Cinema; Aquarium; Bathhouse; Library; Crypt; Park; Recording studio.

SIMPLE BUILDINGS

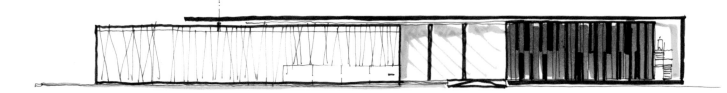

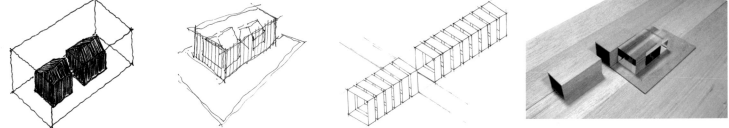

CORPORATE AND MARKETING CENTRE, KOLKATA, INDIA

This development for the Unitech Group is RMJM's first completed project in India. The building functions primarily as an exhibition space to house show flats for Unitech's nearby residential development. The building's private functions (architect's workspace, offices, conference rooms and cafe area) are contained within two solid objects. Local stone and long slender glass windows are layered in a series of horizontal strips like geological strata, emphasising their mass.

The double-height, frameless white box, containing the public functions of the show flats, floats in a reflecting pool and is illuminated from within at night, acting as a beacon in the surrounding landscape.

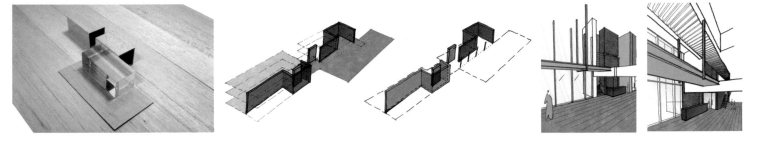

FACING PAGE TOP
Approach elevation
to the east.

FACING PAGE MIDDLE
Initial conceptual
sketches.

FACING PAGE BOTTOM
Sketch studies for
the Indian Pavilion.

TOP
Photographs of
the Pavilion during
construction.

BOTTOM
Sketch and model
studies for the
Indian Pavilion.

SIMPLE BUILDINGS

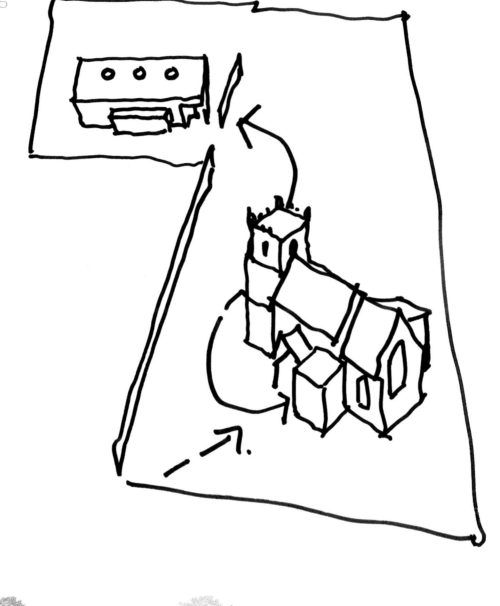

NORTH BUILDING, ALL SAINTS PARISH CHURCH, CAMBRIDGE, UK

This project for an active and growing church in Little
Shelford on the outskirts of Cambridge was the result
of a careful and lengthy process of design and consultation.
Working alongside a building committee chosen from the
congregation, RMJM orchestrated a series of consultation
sessions with English Heritage, the Society for the Protection
of Ancient Buildings, local authority conservation officers and
the village community. Valuable new facilities have been
located in two elements – one attached to the existing
eleventh century listed fabric, and a low, freestanding pavilion
located in a quiet corner of the churchyard.

FACING PAGE TOP
Site sketch showing the
relationship of the new
north building and the
existing church.

FACING PAGE BOTTOM
Elevations.

TOP AND BOTTOM
The simple form and
natural materials make
the scheme an elegant
and sensitive neighbour.

COMPLEX BUILDINGS

COMPLEX BUILDINGS ARE ABOUT SPACE AND THE
LAYERING OF THAT SPACE. EVERY BUILDING HAS A
DEGREE OF INTIMACY, THRESHOLDS OF PUBLIC AND
PRIVATE SPACE, DOORS AND GATES. A HOSPITAL,
LIKE A THEATRE OR A LABORATORY, IS A COMPLEX
BUILDING WITH PLAN DEPTH AND LAYERS OF
ACTIVITY, ACCESSIBILITY AND SECURITY. EVEN A
FAMILY HOUSE CAN BE UNDERSTOOD AS A SPATIALLY
COMPLEX BUILDING WITH ROOMS WITHIN ROOMS
THAT ARE VERY PRIVATE AND OTHER ROOMS THAT
ARE VERY PUBLIC.

LABORATORY OF MOLECULAR BIOLOGY, UK

RMJM's design for this major new laboratory for the
Medical Research Council is based on the principles of
generic planning to provide fully flexible primary laboratories
and write-up areas, linked to a high provision of space for
complex equipment and instrumentation. As with all new
research facilities, the design and layout of the building
is being planned to promote the all important interaction
between research groups. A thorough analysis of work
patterns and circulation routes, linked to a careful
consideration of the location of all shared and social
spaces, has been a primary part of the design development
to ensure that this interaction is 'engineered' to the full.

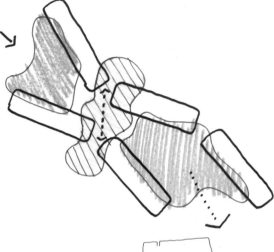

For such an involved
project, a comprehensive
diagrammatic approach
was undertaken.

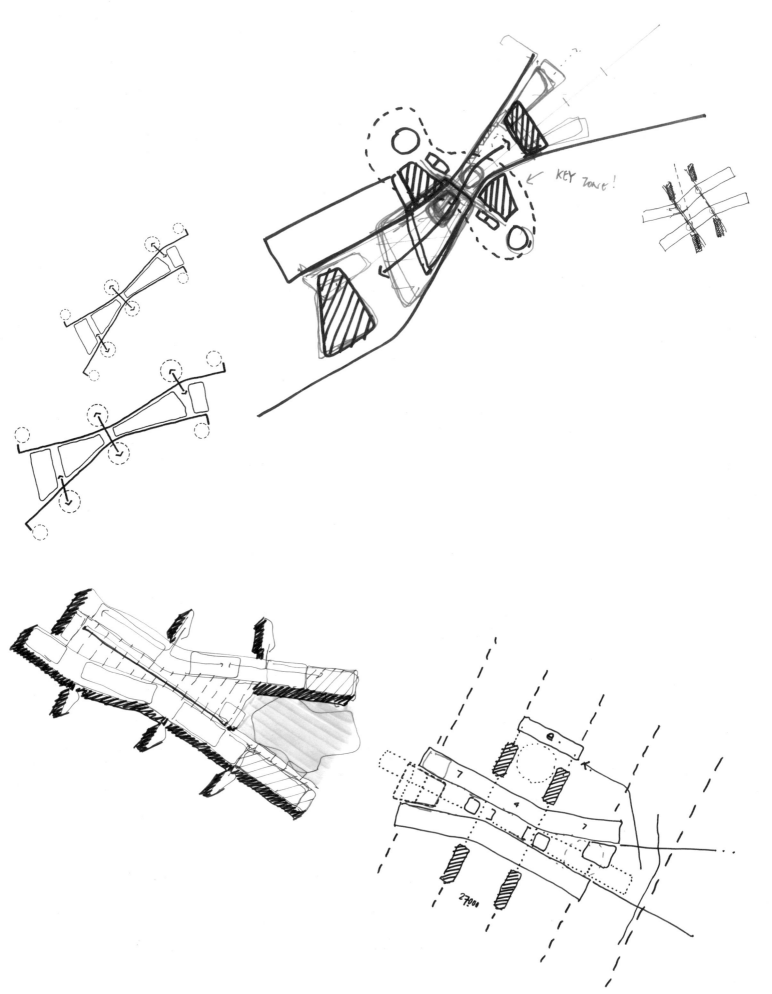

KEY ZONE!

27900

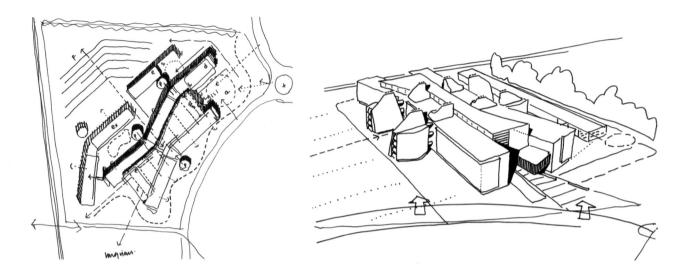

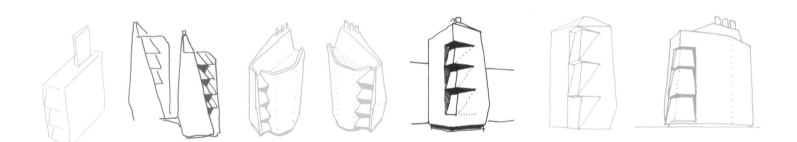

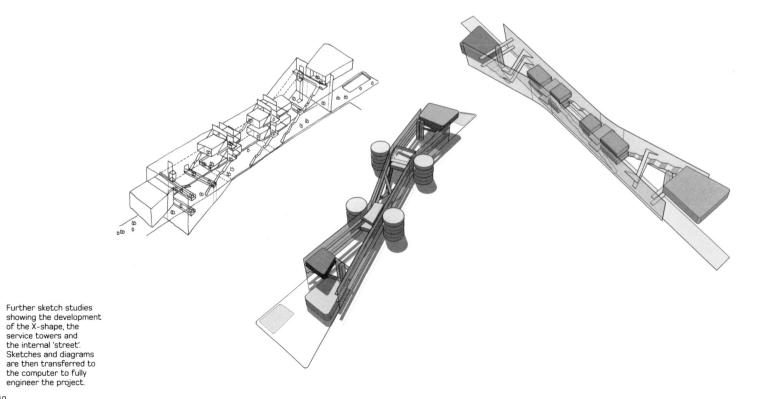

Further sketch studies
showing the development
of the X-shape, the
service towers and
the internal 'street'.
Sketches and diagrams
are then transferred to
the computer to fully
engineer the project.

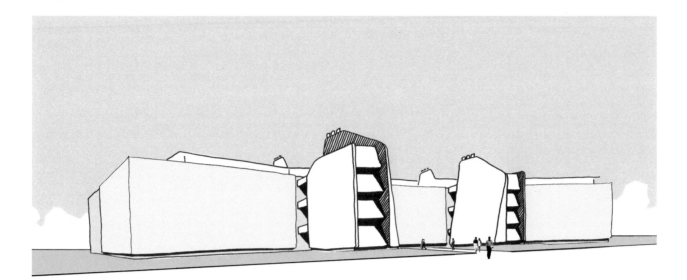

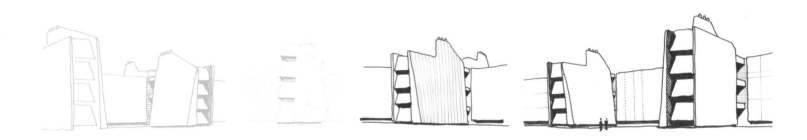

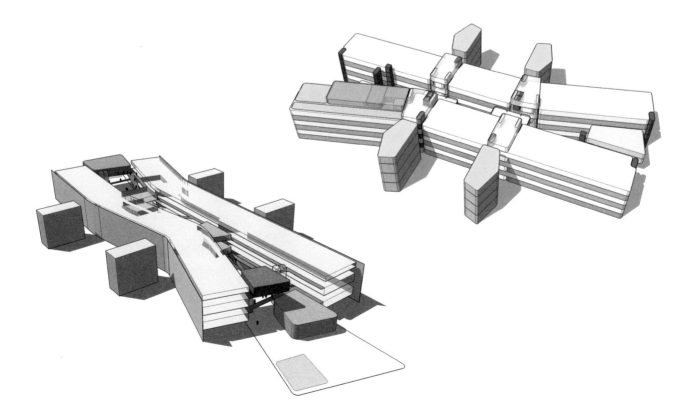

CITY IN THE MICROCOSM
BUILDINGS CAN BE THE HOME FOR SMALL
COMMUNITIES, THEIR INTERNAL CIRCULATION
AND SPACES TAKING ON AN URBAN CHARACTER,
WITH MINI-STREETS AND SQUARES AND MICRO
COMMUNITIES. GOOD ARCHITECTURE WILL
REINFORCE THE POSSIBILITIES LATENT WITHIN
A CLIENT'S BRIEF TO ENCOURAGE A SENSE OF
COMMUNITY WITHIN A BUILDING.

THE TRON THEATRE, GLASGOW, UK

Built in 1795 and surrounded by other Grade A listed
structures, the Tron Kirk has been the subject of a
substantial redevelopment by RMJM. Having rationalised
the planning of these buildings, we set about creating
contemporary and contextual additions. The reimagining
of the foyer with exhibition space, box office, cafe and
auditorium has allowed the development of new activities,
including a studio theatre and administration spaces which
further enhance and develop the role of the theatre.

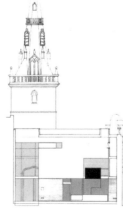
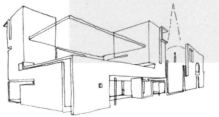
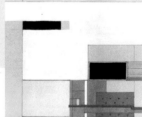

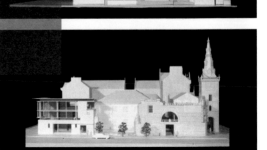

TOP AND BOTTOM
Main image: the box office. Five artists worked with the design team to provide a fusion of art and architecture. This process was highly rewarding and gave an additional layer of complexity to the design.

CITY IN THE MACROCOSM

PLANNING A NEW CITY OR SETTLEMENT ON A SUPER SCALE REQUIRES VISION AND AN EXTRAORDINARY DESIGN COMMITMENT AND UNDERSTANDING OF THE HUMAN CONDITION. WE STRIVE TO CREATE AN EXCITING CONCEPTUAL INFRASTRUCTURE WHERE THE TRANSPORT NETWORKS, LANDSCAPES, FOOTWAYS AND DEVELOPMENT PLOTS ALL COMBINE TO CREATE SOMETHING GREATER THAN THE SUM OF THE PARTS, SETTLEMENTS THAT ARE SUSTAINABLE AND OPTIMISTIC IN THEIR ABILITY TO ACCEPT CHANGE AND STIMULATE OPPORTUNITY FOR EXCITING ARCHITECTURE AND URBAN DESIGN.

CAIRO MASTERPLAN

RMJM's approach to the challenge of raising a new city from more than 100km² of desert on the outskirts of Cairo drew from Egyptian culture and geography. The masterplan design organises the component parts of the city around a metaphoric river, represented by a landscape ribbon running through the site. This ribbon acts as a central focus and links together the different elements of the city, not only providing fantastic amenity space for a population of 800,000 but also accommodating a variety of civic, education and sport campuses along its length. The grain for development around this central space was inspired by the location in the desert and informed by Egyptian environment and ecology. The concept of 'dunes' was directly applied to develop the infrastructural footprint of the masterplan. This approach is based on the notion of a city sculpted from the desert by the natural forces of water and wind.

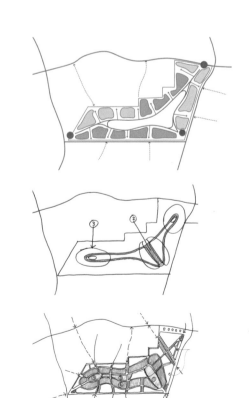

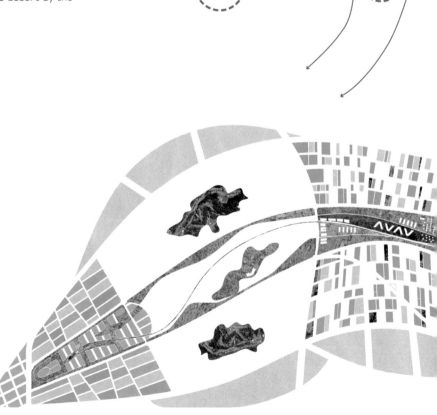

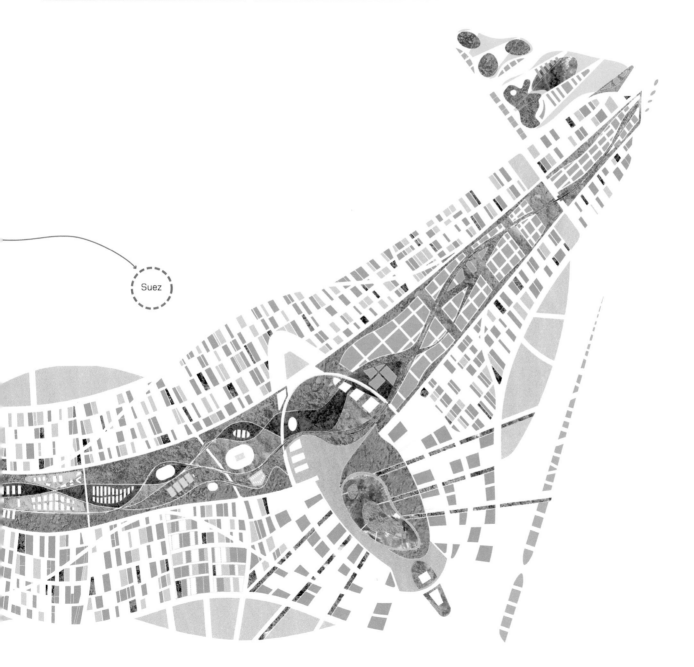

Suez

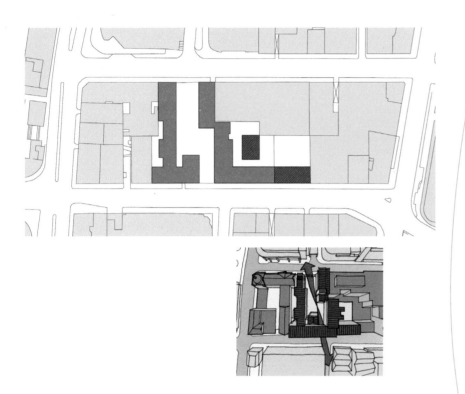

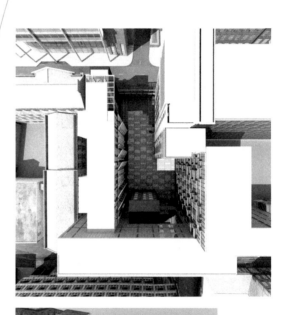

URBAN ROOMS
OUR CITIES' PUBLIC SPACES COULD BE COMPARED
TO A COLLECTION OF LARGE OUTDOOR ROOMS.
WE CAN IMAGINE THESE ROOMS HAVING A SPATIAL
RELATIONSHIP WITH ONE ANOTHER, SOME MORE
PUBLIC THAN OTHERS, WITH THEIR FORM AND
CHARACTER POSITIVELY DEFINED BY URBAN EDGES.
LIKE WALLPAPER IN A ROOM, THE BUILDINGS HELP
TO DEFINE THE CHARACTER OF THE SPACE.

FUSION, GLASGOW, UK

The site for this project bridges an urban block from Oswald
Street to Robertson Street. Following a study of the area's
urban dynamic, RMJM proposed to cut the city block in half in
order to create an enclave for a new urban space and a route
to better connect the area with the city's central shopping
district. The majority of the 200 apartments and commercial
units will enjoy an aspect onto a new public space away from
the busy city streets. RMJM Art Commissioning approached
internationally acclaimed artist Peter McCaughey to design
the courtyard.

FACING PAGE,
CLOCKWISE
FROM TOP LEFT
Plan of the city block
showing the new
public throughway;
Aerial visualisations
of the Oswald Street
'Cut'; Model; Diagram
of the route through
the courtyard.

ABOVE
In working with artist
Peter McCaughey
the Oswald Street
development offers
fascinating challenges in
creating an environment
that addresses the shift
between space that is
fully public, semi-public
and private.

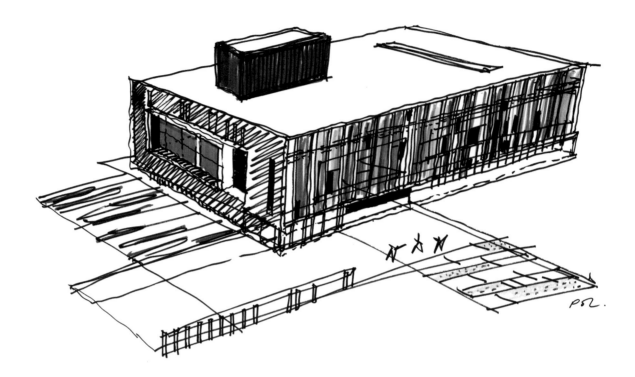

ORGANISATION

A BUILDING'S ORGANISATION REFERS TO THE WAY
IN WHICH ITS MANY PARTS ARE INTERRELATED:
LARGE ROOMS AND SMALL ROOMS; ACTIVITY AND
PROGRAMME; STRUCTURE AND CIRCULATION;
STAIR AND LIFTS; STORAGE AND SERVICE SPACE.
THE COMPLEX MATRIX OF ORGANISING THESE SPACES
AND ACTIVITIES IS CAPTURED IN THE ARCHITECTURAL
DIAGRAM. THE PRIMARY SKILL OF THE ARCHITECT CAN
BE SEEN AS RATIONALISING AND COORDINATING A
COMPLEX KIT OF PARTS INTO THE ARCHITECTURAL
DIAGRAM WHICH WILL ULTIMATELY DEFINE THE
ESSENTIAL ARCHAEOLOGY OF A PROPOSAL.

**THE PERFORMANCE ACADEMY,
NEWCASTLE COLLEGE, UK**

This unique creative hub provides students with world class facilities, consistent with the outstanding teaching and learning that has been demonstrated at the school in recent years. The building's programme is split into two parts. To the rear is a large metal clad box containing large span spaces: a 250-seat theatre; a 200 capacity music venue; TV studio; recording studios; acting and dance centres. Many of these are 'black box' spaces which require little or no daylight with the exception of the six dance studios, located on th[e] floor, which benefit from natural overhead light. To th[e] front of the building there is a 'light box', a glazed str[ucture] containing smaller spaces such as classrooms, semin[ar] and staff rooms enjoying daylight and natural ventila[tion]. This structure spans 70 metres using a polycarbonat[e] exoskeleton truss. The dramatic space created below[is] the building's entrance and front of house foyer.

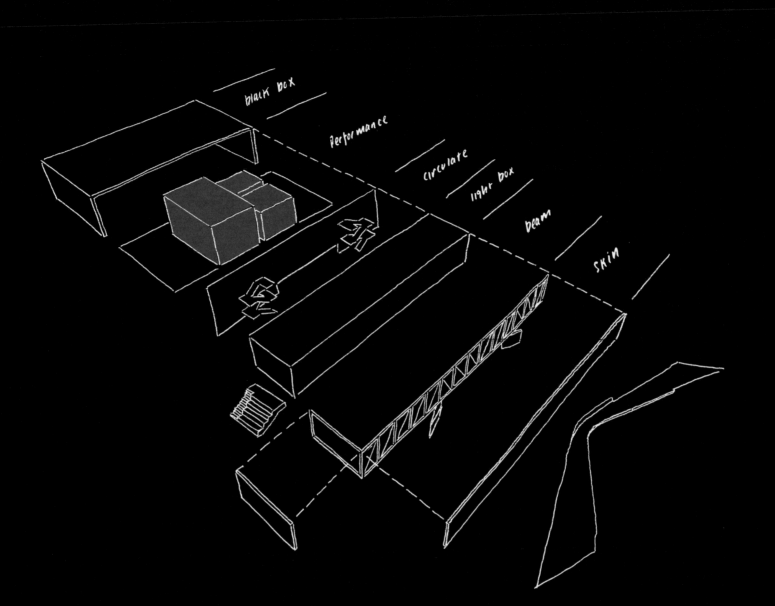

black box

Performance

circulate

light box

beam

skin

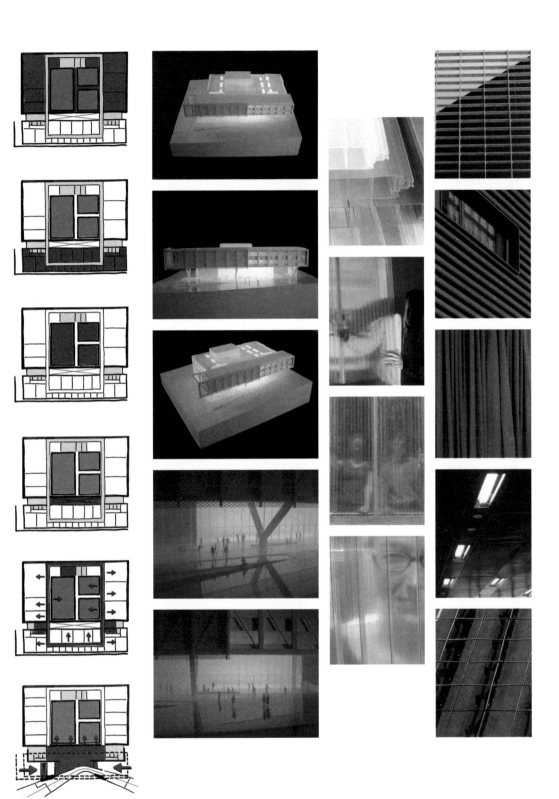

COLUMNS, FROM LEFT
Sketches showing the
organisation of spaces
in red. From top:
acoustic buffering,
light box, acoustic-
sensitive, in-between
space, circulation space,
front of house;

Study models;
The design team
investigates the opacity
of their polycarbonate
samples; Interior and
exterior finish details.

FACING PAGE TOP
Night-time exterior,
north elevation.

FACING PAGE BOTTOM
FROM LEFT
The exterior cantilever
polycarbonate skin, interior
finishing in the studios
and 250-seat theatre.

MACHINES AND SYSTEMS
IMAGINATIVELY CONSIDERING THE BUILDING'S SUPPORT SYSTEMS, ITS SKELETON, ITS ESSENTIAL ORGANS AND CIRCULATION.

ANCILLARY SPACE

MECHANICAL SYSTEMS

STRUCTURE, SYSTEMS AND SPACE
AS NATURAL COLLABORATORS, RMJM BELIEVES THAT SUCCESSFUL ARCHITECTURE SHOULD BE A DEMONSTRABLE FUSION OF STRUCTURE, SYSTEMS AND SPACE. WE HAVE ALWAYS STRIVEN TO DELIVER SOLUTIONS FOR OUR CLIENTS WHICH CAREFULLY INTEGRATE STRUCTURE WITH ENVIRONMENTAL AND SPATIAL DEMANDS TO CREATE SIMPLE, FLEXIBLE ACCOMMODATION.

STRUCTURAL SYSTEMS

The primary drivers are simple: floor depths which enable daylight to flood the space, minimising energy consumption; atrium spaces which act as environmental mediators as well as nodes of social activity; and circulation routes which respond naturally to the occupiers' daily pattern of work and life.

The plans opposite illustrate some of our family of projects.

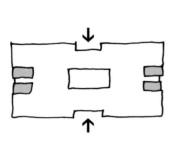
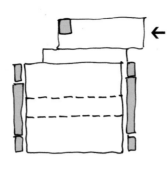
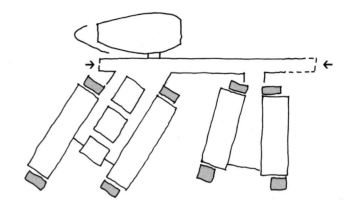

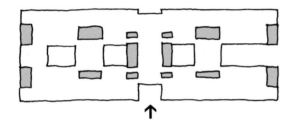
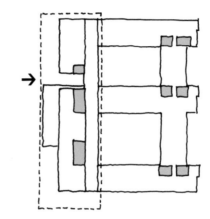
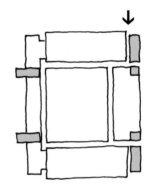

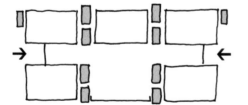
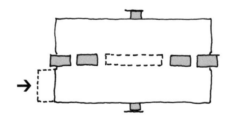
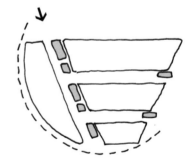

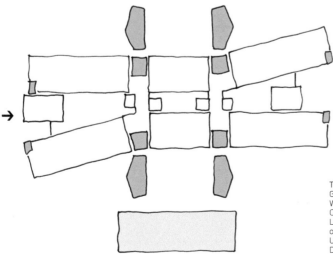

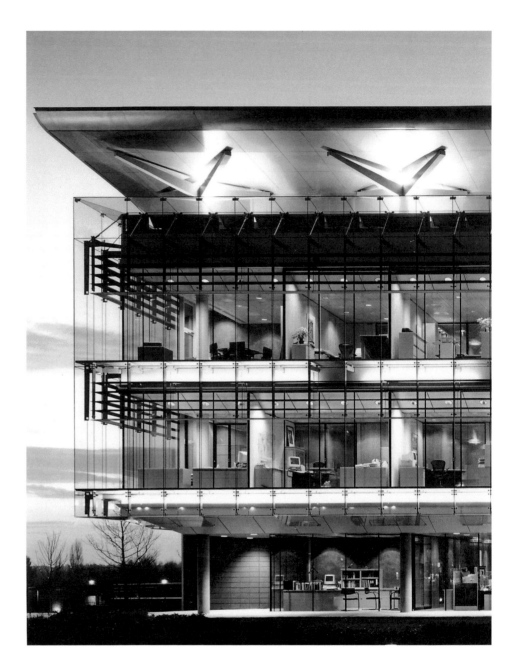

CONSTRUCTIONAL SYSTEMS
CONTEMPORARY BUILDINGS HAVE A LAYERING
OF DIFFERENT BUILDING SYSTEMS AND
CONSTRUCTION TECHNIQUES.

Supported by its superstructure, a building has both primary
and secondary constructions. Primary construction relates to
the major building components of the walls, roofs and floors,
while secondary construction relates to non-structural
internal walls and fitments. A skilful architect will thoroughly
exploit the qualities of each of these layers, understanding
that each has a unique opportunity to add richness and
meaning to the architecture.

TOP FROM LEFT
A further selection of
construction finishes:
Copper, terracotta, brass.

SECOND ROW
FROM LEFT
Cement, profiled metal,
fibre cement.

THIRD ROW FROM LEFT
Cedar wood, terracotta,
polycarbonate.

BOTTOM
Stone.

FACING PAGE
Glaxo Wellcome World
Headquarters, London,
showing various layers of
construction technique.

ANCILLARY SPACE
LIFTS, STAIRS, RAMPS, CUPBOARDS, TOILETS, KITCHENS, PLANT ROOMS AND FIREPLACES ARE AMONG THE SERVICE TYPE ACCOMMODATION THAT WE WOULD DESCRIBE AS ANCILLARY.

RATHER THAN SEE THIS TYPE OF ACCOMMODATION AS UNINTERESTING, AN IMAGINATIVE ARCHITECT WOULD CONSIDER THE POTENTIAL THIS TYPE OF SPACE HAS FOR ARTICULATING AND DIFFERENTIATING A NEW ARCHITECTURE.

FACULTY OF EDUCATION, UNIVERSITY OF GLASGOW, UK

Completely reversing the building and creating a 'battery pack' extension was RMJM's response to the brief to refurbish an imposing, red sandstone building for Glasgow University. The new building contains the main entrance, social areas and vertical circulation. All floors of the existing building tie through those of the 'battery pack', with a horizontal loop providing an orientation reference point at each level. The new entrance is located two floors below the original entrance level, opening up a whole new space on the lower floors that was previously under-utilised.

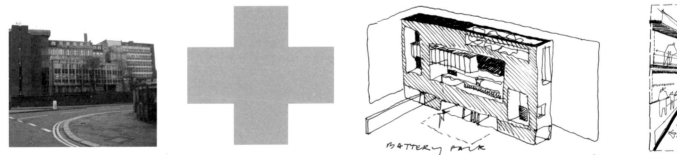

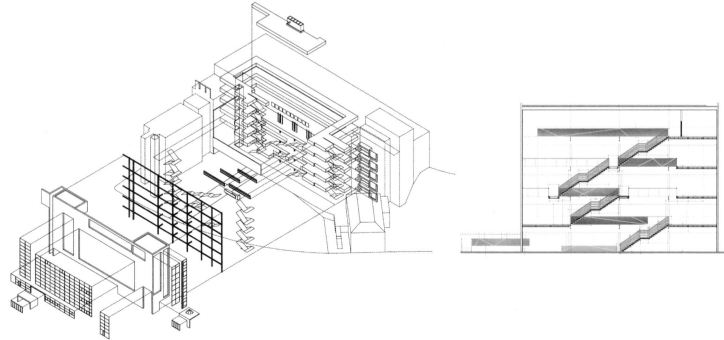

A variety of imagery illustrating the design evolution for the 'battery pack'.

MECHANICAL SYSTEMS
BEFORE ANY STRATEGIC DECISIONS CAN BE MADE, ARCHITECTS NEED TO KNOW HOW THEIR PROPOSED ENVIRONMENTS WILL PERFORM. THAT'S WHY IT IS ESSENTIAL THAT ARCHITECTS HAVE A GOOD UNDERSTANDING OF THE 'DYNAMICS OF MECHANICS'.

THIS ENCOMPASSES KNOWLEDGE SUCH AS HOW PASSIVE VENTILATION STRATEGIES AND AIR FLOW MIGHT WORK IN A NEW OFFICE BUILDING' TO HOW HEAT GAINS IN CONCRETE MIGHT AFFECT THE ROOM TEMPERATURES IN A NEW SCHOOL. ARCHITECTS, AS LATERAL THINKERS WORKING IN TANDEM WITH CREATIVE ENGINEERS, CAN QUITE LITERALLY REINVENT THE WHEEL.

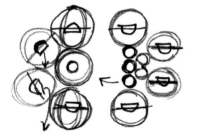

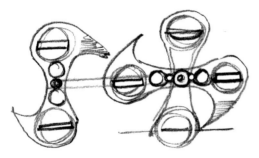

Development sketches illustrating the cog formation and CAD drawings.

THE FALKIRK WHEEL, UK

The functional brief for the Falkirk Wheel was to take two boats up and two boats down the 35-metre vertical drop between the Forth and Clyde Canals in 15 minutes. RMJM rejected the previous design concepts, which in general were based around a Ferris wheel-type structure, in favour of a design that would have as its basis a true understanding of the massive symbolic and artistic potential of such an important project. This understanding was reflected in the way in which the wheel form was reinterpreted to create a unique and memorable solution. All RMJM's design proposals went back to the same basic question – how to raise and lower boats quickly while celebrating the joining of the two canals in a manner befitting the new millennium. This resulted in a wide variety of ideas, from simple engineering structures to a purely aesthetic approach where the actual engineering was immersed within a larger artistic concept. Interestingly, the winning design looks to do both, combining art and engineering.

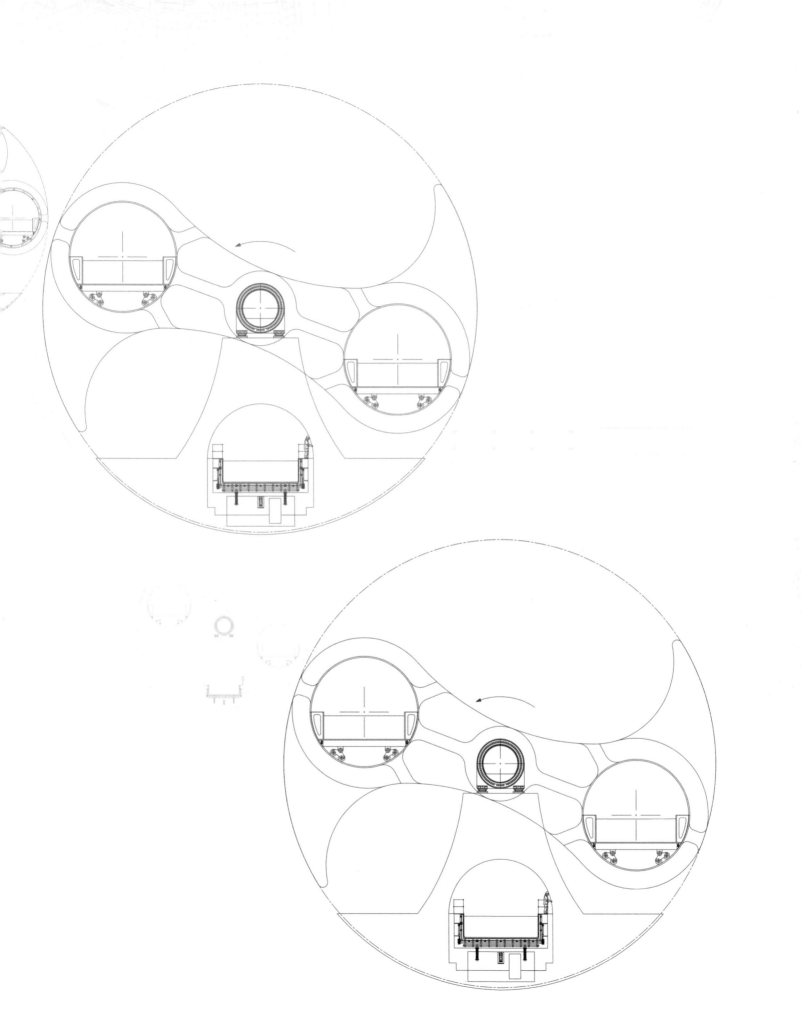

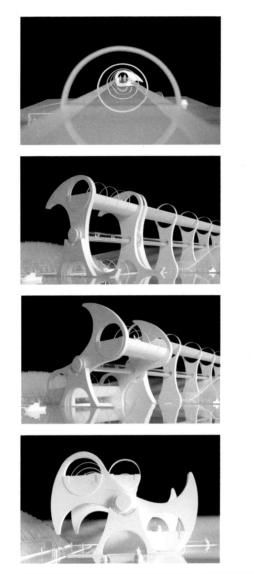

TOP
Model work.

BOTTOM
The wheel in motion
with the visitor centre
looking on.

FACING PAGE
Closer shot of the wheel
workings and the cedar
wood visitor centre.

LOW ENERGY AND ENVIRONMENTAL SYSTEMS

THE ZUCKERMAN INSTITUTE FOR CONNECTIVE
ENVIRONMENTAL RESEARCH (ZICER) IS A HIGHER
EDUCATION ESTABLISHMENT UNITING FIVE RESEARCH
CENTRES FROM THE UNIVERSITY OF EAST ANGLIA'S
INTERNATIONALLY-ACCLAIMED SCHOOL OF
ENVIRONMENTAL SCIENCES.

IN AN INSTITUTE DEDICATED TO THE STUDY OF
ENVIRONMENTAL CHALLENGES, IT WAS VITAL TO
SHOWCASE THIS RESEARCH ACTIVITY BY APPLYING
ENVIRONMENTAL DESIGN PRINCIPLES TO THE
NEW BUILDING.

AS WELL AS INSULATION AND AIR TIGHTNESS LEVELS
WHICH SURPASS THOSE REQUIRED BY BUILDING
REGULATIONS, THE PLAN LAYOUT MAXIMISES
DAYLIGHT AND PROVIDES A COMBINATION OF
NATURAL AND FORCED VENTILATION WHICH UTILISES
THE THERMAL MASS OF THE FABRIC. PHOTOVOLTAIC
PANELS HAVE BEEN USED FOR THE ROOF LEVEL
EXHIBITION AND LECTURE SPACES.

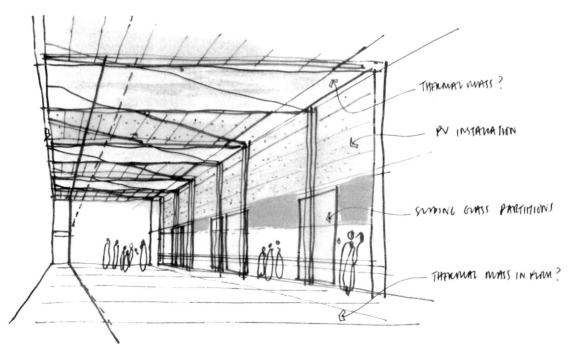

THERMAL MASS ?

PV INSTALLATION

SLIDING GLASS PARTITIONS

THERMAL MASS IN PLAN ?

RIGHT
Illustration of the ZICER
project's environmental
components.

FACING PAGE
ZICER main entrance.

SUMMARY OF ENERGY CONSUMPTION FIGURES FOR THE
ZUCKERMAN INSTITUTE FOR CONNECTIVE ENVIRONMENTAL RESEARCH:

MEASURED AIR
LEAKAGE RATE AT
COMPLETION:
2.85m³/hr per m² of
permeable envelope at
a maintained pressure
difference of 50 Pa.

U-VALUES:
windows	1.0 W/m2 K
walls	0.2 W/m2 K
roof	1.3 W/m2 K
floor	1.6 W/m2 K

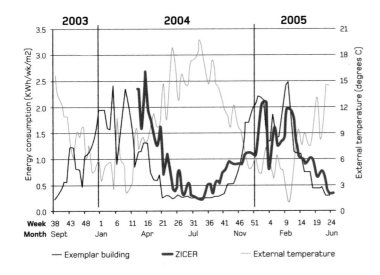

GAS CONSUMPTION (heating and hot water)

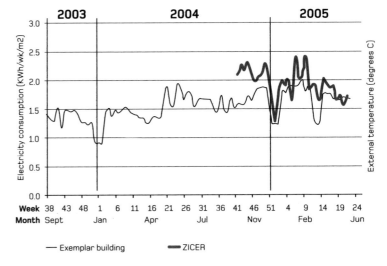

ELECTRICITY CONSUMPTION

JULIET LANDLER, DANA RAYDAN AND PETER WILLIAMS
GOOD DESIGN IS SUSTAINABLE DESIGN

The urban planners, landscape architects and architects at RMJM recognise the fundamental relationship between architecture and the deterioration of the environment.

Designing and constructing buildings and cities contributes significantly to the global problems of habitat destruction and loss of bio-diversity, global warming, ozone depletion, soil erosion, acid rain, air pollution, water pollution, soil pollution, toxic waste and the depletion of freshwater supplies and mineral reserves. It is architecture – commercial, industrial, and residential buildings – that accounts for half of all energy consumed.

The practice's underlying philosophy today is that our architects and planners design to meet each client's specific needs, rather than to follow dogmatically any specific architectural style. This approach has led to a rich tapestry of RMJM buildings that have stood the test of time. While we take considerable pride in our early projects, in more recent years we have realised that having the ability to create buildings that endure well is only a critical first step towards sustainability.

In order to create the architecture of the future, architecture that is truly healthy for both people and the Earth, we must all improve and change our current working methods and improve the buildings and cities we create.

We have been studying how RMJM's buildings have performed since their construction. At the University of East Anglia, for example, we measured our buildings' energy performance on campus. The results (shown above), presented at the Passive and Low Energy Architecture (PLEA) Conference in 2005, showed that although the buildings were amongst the lowest for energy use of their type in the country, they were still not performing as well as we thought they would. By using the results of our analysis, however, we are now working with the client and users to develop a strategy to reduce energy use even further on campus.

RMJM has also been instrumental, with a group of like-minded clients and consultants, in research we've called 'Soft Landings'. This is intended to help the client immediately prior to, and post, the handover of the building.

Occupiers need to know how to use and run the building to ensure maximum performance. It sounds very obvious but often the client moves in and then struggles to control the building. Communication about simple issues – turning off lights, putting blinds down on hot afternoons – allows the building users control of their own environment and the psychological benefits that arise out of that control, together with the benefits of a better internal environment.

Our 50th anniversary also sees the launch of RMJM's environmental design group, which offers a separate client-focused service, advising on how to reduce energy expenditures and environmental impacts in existing property portfolios and estates management practice, as well on new build projects for RMJM and other consultants and clients.

This group will complement the role of RMJM's environmental assessors, who already have extensive experience in Building Research Establishment's Environmental Assessment Method (BREEAM) and Leadership in Energy and Environmental Design's (LEED) green building rating systems assessments,

and who operate in the UK and across Asia. The environmental design group, like the rest of RMJM, will work with quality management systems to ensure that the lessons learnt across our projects from around the world are fed back into RMJM via our intranet system so that all our staff can benefit from the experience.

As designers, we embrace our role in meeting the challenges posed by the environmental crisis. With our portfolio of projects and extensive international experience, we look forward to being influential, active players in creating the innovative architectural systems and methods that will make our future works truly sustainable.

Our Cambridge office in the UK is low-lying and threatened by rising sea levels. We will be able to measure our success in 2056 – RMJM's centenary year – by whether we still cycle to work or have to use canoes.

ZICER won *Building Design's* Low Energy Building of the Year award in 2005.

ROBERT MATTHEW, *CHARCOAL ON PAPER*, 1960

DESIGN
INTUITION AND RATIONALE

ROBERT MATTHEW, *CHARCOAL ON PAPER*, 1961

IDEAS AND CONCEPTS
DESIGN REQUIRES THAT YOU TAKE A LEAP OF FAITH
AND COMMIT TO AN IDEA, A CONCEPT AND A STARTING
POINT. RARELY IS THIS STARTING POINT ENTIRELY
RATIONAL BUT RATHER INTUITIVE AND INSPIRED
BY SEEMINGLY UNRELATED CONCEPTS. OUR MASTER-
PLANS AND BUILDINGS MIGHT LOOK TO STRUCTURES
AND FORMS FOUND IN NATURE. WHAT IS IMPORTANT
IS THAT THE ESSENTIAL CONCEPT IS EMBEDDED
IN THE DESIGN SO THAT WE MIGHT CREATE
A MEANINGFUL ARCHITECTURAL LANGUAGE.
OUR GOAL IS TO PUT ART INTO ARCHITECTURE.

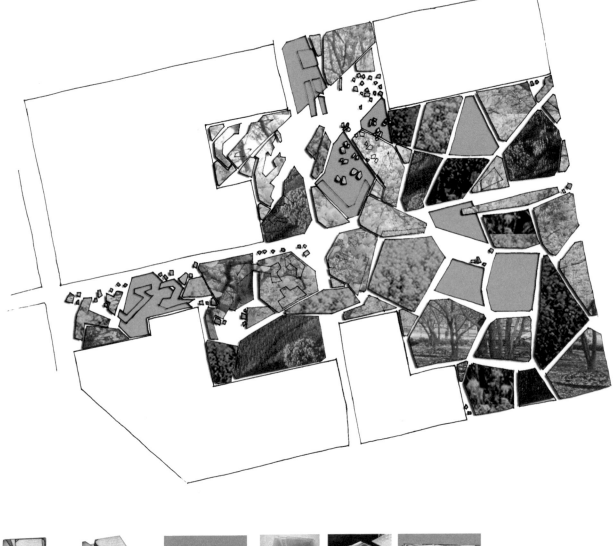

LANGFANG MASTERPLAN, CHINA

The city of Langfang, located between Beijing and Tian Jing, has a population of nearly four million people. RMJM's masterplan for a new district in the city will provide 820 high quality residential units including villas with communal and private gardens and a cultural hub for the city's growing population. The design inspiration for the 160 acre site originates from images of cracked glaciers. Within the masterplan, these cracked lines form the road network and pathways whilst the remaining glacier pieces form 'islands' accommodating a mix of uses across the site. The creation of the new cultural and leisure hub in Langfang aims to encourage the financial and commercial development of the new central business district and the nature of the design and the facilities has already attracted substantial interest, including four major Chinese banking institutions and a five star international hotel chain.

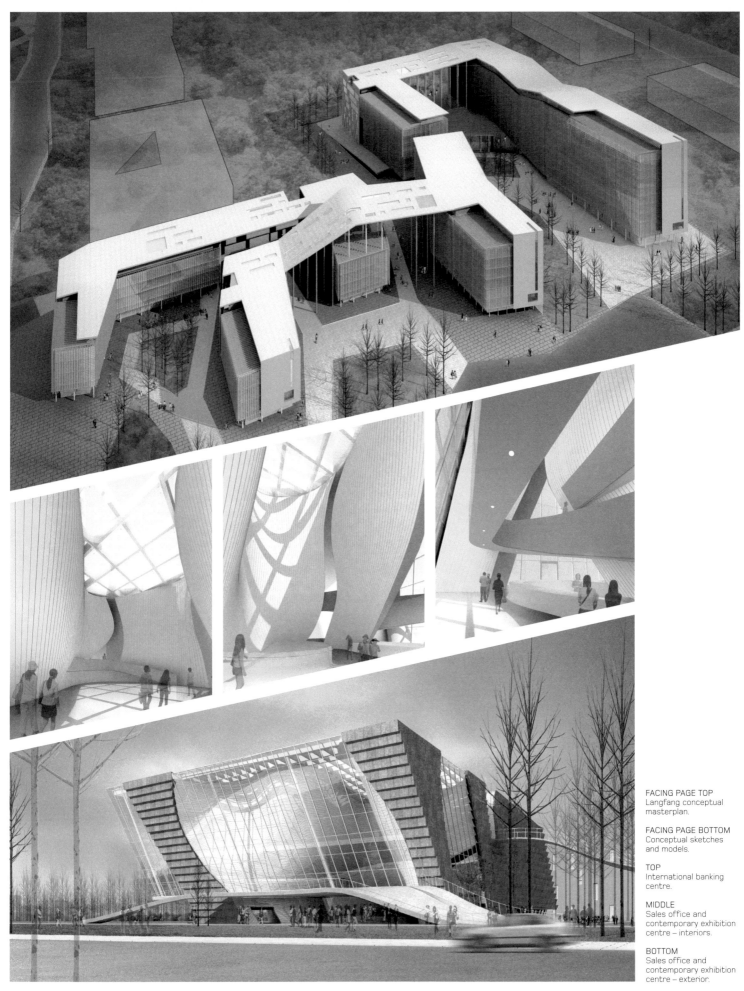

FACING PAGE TOP
Langfang conceptual
masterplan.

FACING PAGE BOTTOM
Conceptual sketches
and models.

TOP
International banking
centre.

MIDDLE
Sales office and
contemporary exhibition
centre – interiors.

BOTTOM
Sales office and
contemporary exhibition
centre – exterior.

"... HE PRODUCED AN IMPORTANT BODY OF MODERNIST OIL PAINTINGS.... THE WORKS ON PAPER AND THE WORKS ON CANVAS DISPLAY A THOROUGH UNDERSTANDING OF THE MODERN MOVEMENT AND REFLECT THE SAME AESTHETIC CONCERNS AS HIS FRIENDS AND COLLEAGUES LE CORBUSIER, PICASSO AND MOORE."
EXTRACT FROM EXHIBITION CATALOGUE, 'SIR ROBERT MATTHEW, A SECRET PASSION', 1906 – 1975

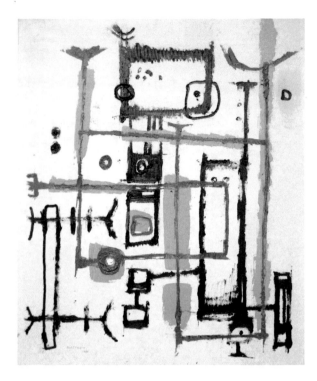

PAUL STALLAN
PAINTING AS A LABORATORY OF FORM

INTUITIVE CONFIDENCE REQUIRES PRACTICE
Although I have been painting similar shapes and forms for the past 15 years, I have never really analysed them as a body of work, rather just enjoyed the process of making them. Looking back I can trace common shapes and patterns. It is as though my brain has a 'muscle memory' that prescribes a family of forms and related images. When I start a new canvas I throw paint at the surface and with the addition of more paint layers seek to post-rationalise and compose the emerging patterns and figurative shapes that appear. I have developed a 'language' it seems, an internal language which is a dialogue between favoured shapes.

My painting 'language' has been inspired by constant doodling of structural forms, 'ship' shapes and 'submarines', with architectural grids overlaid with flexible skins and masks – a playground of personal and visual ideas.

These experiments in paint are like micro-architectural composition, free from any functional requirement, warm-up exercises; like a gymnast free-styling and practising potential moves before a public presentation, they are mental gymnastics and always work-in-progress.

To develop a visual intelligence and I guess to maintain a keen eye requires a constant investment and exploration. Intuitive confidence requires practice.

SUBMARINE SKINS
The 'architectural skins' that I draw in my paintings adopt various 'submarine-like' configurations, they can be seen as hung, or to act like a cladding or wrap, they can seal a form or space, they can also be cut and punctured and peppered with holes. These skins that I detail I imagine are like an abstract representation of say a metal rain screen, an architectural thinness that protects like a waterproof jacket. Or they can be more like the hull of a ship or a submarine or like a skin of concrete covering a landscape. Whatever

form the layers of paint take, these 'skins' have one thing in common and that is that I always imagine them being defensive, protecting us from the rain, shielding us from noise, blocking the sun, creating imagined interior and exterior relationships.

The shapes I make are fluid and figurative and help me to imagine a contemporary and responsive vernacular that I might use in my architecture.

STRUCTURAL GAMES
A structural shape or figure or families of structural forms are generally always apparent; i.e. shapes that help me compose my paintings and allow the secondary forms and characters within my compositions to find their place. The structural shapes represent actual structural systems that you might encounter in a building, or a crane, or a bridge.

THE IMPORTANCE OF PAINT AS A MEDIUM
The purpose and the influence of painting and its relationship to practice as an architect is for me not a direct one. My paintings are not representations or abstractions of any particular landscape or building but rather of an imaginary place. The figures and forms are recycled forms that I might use in part in a future design, forms that I have seen elsewhere that I am reconfiguring, or simply shapes that I like which have emerged from the canvas. Using paint as a medium to explore these ideas on shape is like a forensic process, answers are revealed through a form of analysis.

As an architect there is a wide choice of techniques to help me sketch and model ideas, from a soft lead pencil to sophisticated 3-D computer modelling packages. It is however the unpredictability and liquidity of paint as a material that has a special interest. I am completely absorbed, when painting, in the detail of how the paint will react and what control I can exert over it given. It seems to develop a life of its own.

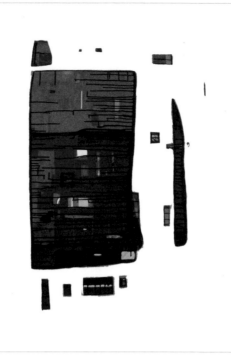
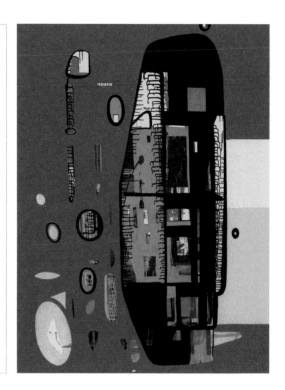

It is this lack of control over the fluidity of the paint and the hit-and-miss marks on the canvas which pose the challenge. It is like a competition between my rational mind and the unpredictability of the paint, the paint sometimes winning by undoing a composition that took a lot of time. When I 'win' with a paint layer, it means the colour contrasts and shape relations within the painting somehow work for me.

At times a canvas can also get 'too busy'. Each of the shapes and patterns may be interesting in isolation but don't work in combination. To paint over them can be painful but the achievement of getting the whole canvas working together is the primary objective.

Being able to throw paint onto the canvas and post-rationalise and massage the marks did not come naturally initially. I blame my architectural education to some extent, which did not encourage more intuitive study. When it comes to form-making, architectural education tends to promote formulaic or prescriptive methods with academic analysis and theory. Architecture courses tend to study the dynamics of form in a dispassionate and detached fashion which probably make it easier to teach than in a more open-ended, experimental aesthetics programme which encourages students to discover form, colour and shape for themselves.

It was not until late on in my education that I was encouraged to be more experimental. I have tried subsequently to extend this studio-based learning experience by building on the scientific and artistic perspectives of art and form and comparing and contrasting these two opposites against each other; i.e. the rational and the intuitive.

My explorations in paint are useful at a fundamental level to me as an architect. Understanding not only how the dynamics of a form or colour can benefit design, but also to have the confidence and ability to experiment and discover these forms and shapes intuitively is exciting and constantly challenging.

I recently received an invitation to the opening of a small exhibition of drawings and paintings by the late Robert Matthew (a founding partner of RMJM), the invitation sent on to me by his family. The exhibition was entitled 'A Secret Passion', the work having never been publicly exhibited.

I had not realised that Matthew had ever prepared a canvas and was excited to learn more about his painting and how it might reveal more about his practice as an architect. What was a real surprise were the parallels I could make between Sir Robert's paintings and my own, both in terms of why he made them and for their architectural character.

I re-read the preceding text which I wrote for this publication before seeing the Matthew exhibition. In it I had explored the intuitive connections between my paintings and the forms I made as an architect. Now, after seeing the show I am even more convinced of the benefits of figurative and formal exploration through drawings.

FACING PAGE
Painting by Robert Matthew from the 1950s.

TOP FROM LEFT
Paintings by Paul Stallan; Defensible or paranoid towerhouse; Building stretch marks; Vertical submarine building.

WHAT USE IS A BOOK WITHOUT
PICTURES OR CONVERSATIONS?

INNOVATION IS REQUIRED IN EVERYTHING WE
DO AS DESIGNERS, FROM NEW URBAN PATTERNS
TO THE SMALLEST ELEMENT OF A BUILDING'S
CONSTRUCTION. WITHOUT IT THERE IS NO PROGRESS
AND ULTIMATELY NO CULTURAL DEVELOPMENT.

TONY KETTLE
NEW FORMS IN ARCHITECTURE

RMJM is an architectural practice that promotes a
collaborative design approach, offering clients an opportunity
to partner and develop projects through a dynamic process
of refining the brief. Areas of innovation can be sought and
tested in order to find the best solutions for the client.
We are international architects but we don't have an obvious
'international style'. We have an interest in the specific –
the client, the climate, the culture. We pursue design that
responds to every unique project, environment and brief and
we look for opportunities to create quality in each layer or
element of design, from urban design to a building detail.

Clients seek value in architectural, environmental or monetary
terms. They look to maximise their returns and seek the
optimum for the cost of any project. Design ideas unlock
problems, but real value comes from innovative thinking that
can unlock the underlying, the hidden, the unexpected or help
a building to perform better given a changing environment.
It is this innate value that we search for.

To innovate you must wonder if there is a better way – the status quo may not be the best way. Experience is valuable if used in the correct way, but just as it can inform solutions it can inhibit new thinking. What is important is the desire to understand every aspect of a problem and a real will to discover opportunities for foresight. Design can readily comply with an existing code, but energy taxes, for example, are probably just around the corner. By 'redesigning' the brief through asking more pertinent questions at every stage of the process, we can discover the client's real requirements. We get better answers as a result.

The risk implicit in innovation can be of a controlled variety. RMJM has used tried and tested concepts and technologies, putting them together in new ways to create new solutions. Products which are already licensed can be adapted without the need for expensive recertification. When new products or technologies are required our in-house research and development unit can prototype and test solutions before

use. This approach has the potential to create a complex and ever-expanding architectural language without exposing clients to unnecessary risk. One example of this approach was the Halo light fitting we designed for a client (pictured opposite). This circular fitting allowed both up and down lighting and also accommodated an air-conditioning vent, which provided the visual advantage of removing unsightly vents while simultaneously providing more local control of the air-conditioning system and the ability to include more cellular offices in the building.

The construction of a building is the construction of a prototype, a one off, never to be repeated. Whilst later buildings might share some of the same elements, unless the project is prefabricated, it will be a prototype. The construction industry expects each prototype to work first time with few if any problems, an assumption based on the experience and skill of the designer and construction team. But as each project is a prototype, it is also a piece of innovation.

If traditional construction or tried and tested technology is employed the risks will be reduced, but the skill is really in how the technology of separate parts work together. At Newcastle College we were able, for example, to use our knowledge of how components fitted together, to place a translucent plastic screen in front of a traditional glazed curtain wall. This allowed the new plastic screen to carry images and be lit from behind, creating a vibrant contemporary abstract artwork.

We are also seeing opportunities for innovation in how society functions. 'Sustainable' has become a catch-all description for things that range from low-energy, to recycling and transport, but the ultimate goal is the 'sustainable community': this is a community that can continuously reinvent itself, finding a balance not only with nature and the physical environment, but also with new industries and changes in the local economy. The challenge here for architects is to facilitate the ability to adapt, and design-in as robust a future as possible. At Leith Docks in Edinburgh a new community is being created out of a former industrial zone. RMJM's plan builds on the advantage of the

waterfront environment with new tourism and leisure hubs, including social and cultural facilities incorporating Leith's maritime heritage by reinventing building uses.

The new emphasis on sustainability is encouraging innovation in new building types. These may be born from a marriage of existing uses, but they become more than the sum of their parts, creating their own unique character. They have the potential to enrich our lives by challenging our perspective of the status quo and expanding our understanding of what society really needs.

At Woodhorn in Northumberland, the Old Ashington coal pit was declared a Scheduled Ancient Monument, but instead of simply restoring the old pithead buildings, they now house the 'Pitman Paintings', an art collection of colliers' art and have been combined with new contemporary buildings that also house an archive of the pit community – births, deaths, marriages – keeping alive the memory of a community. The local community can also use the buildings for 'mat-making' a local craft, which miners' families pursue and can now be carried on in what is effectively a new 'town hall'.

Looking at architecture as a whole, we can see that it has evolved through a series of pragmatic and stylistic phases affected but not limited by:

· the celebration of construction and materials;
· the importance of use, the individual building;
· local community and the collective;
· civilised society and its myriad organisations such as democracy and religion;
· the underlying balance of nature;
· the organised 'chaos' of the universe.

New forms of architecture are always possible due to improvements in technology, as illustrated by historical precedent. New forms are also possible due to freedom of thought, perhaps especially now there is no one doctrine which drives architecture. Instead, we are in a period where individual expression is possible. This is not limited to an individual artistic response, but rather there is the opportunity to reflect the culture of our society and make architecture accessible to everyone – architecture that is thoughtful, inventive and understandable.

What sort of responses can we expect in contemporary architecture?
· Functional Response – the pragmatic brief encompassing spaces standards and spatial relationships.
· Technical Response – the use of technology to achieve or exceed building standards.
· Climatic response – an understanding of climatic conditions and environmental factors affecting a building form.
· Contextual response – an understanding of what is special about the 'place' in terms of site, materials, grain, massing, and history.
· Symbolic Response – in the tradition of modernism, architects attempted to respond rigorously to the concept of "form follows function". This meaning of 'function' was limited to that of pragmatic, physical use. But surely architecture is about so much more than just 'functional building'. It encompasses the artistic, the symbolic, the spiritual. It must include the function of art and demonstrate some ability to resonate at an emotional or spiritual level.

"LIKE ALL FORMS OF CIVILISATION, ARCHITECTURAL DEVELOPMENT HAS FOR CENTURIES MOVED FROM HOMOGENEITY TO HETEROGENEITY... TO BE TRUE, ARCHITECTURE MUST NORMALLY EXPRESS THE CONDITIONS OF LIFE ABOUT AND WITHIN IT, NOT IN A FRAGMENTARY AND SPASMODIC WAY, BUT IN THE MASS AND STRUCTURE, THE LIFE OF THE BUILDING IN LARGE AND COMPREHENSIVE TYPE."

John Root

ROGER WHITEMAN
OFFICES AS AN EXPRESSION OF TIME

When John Root, the architect of the Monadnock building in Chicago, 1892, said this, he was suggesting that the facts of an age, in his case the age of steam, of electricity, of gas, plumbing, sanitation, should be expressed in a new art, the art of building. Building as a physical expression that should reflect the times we live in, and as an art form that shapes our lives, the way we live, how and where we work and what we do when we put our feet up in the evenings.

His comments can be simplified to a single phrase: Architecture is an expression of our time.

This essay does not focus on specific client requirements, new trends in office development and space usage, or the whims of architects, but it questions, on a philosophical level, whether the office is an expression of our time.

In order to evaluate the impact our environment has on office buildings and vice versa, we asked ourselves three questions to see if a trend could be established and new trends predicted:
· What is the structure of a good office building?
· How is the structure affected by time?
· Can conclusions be drawn to influence the next generation of office buildings?

WHAT IS THE STRUCTURE OF A GOOD OFFICE BUILDING?
In discussions with developers, occupiers, agents, consultants and others in the UK, USA, Germany and Holland, it became clear that there are three common strands running through all projects. We see this as a basic molecular structure, with individual cells that grow and change to determine the characteristics of specific projects.

At the core of the structure are the 'briefing cells', a random set of cells typically the same for each project but emphasised with different levels of importance. These include construction budget, net-to-gross ratios, open-plan and cellular spaces, natural ventilation/comfort cooling, and many others.

Providing order around this set of briefing cells is a tight-fitting ring of regulatory cells and control systems. These put order into the molecular structure ensuring the briefing cells do not undermine the control systems. The regulatory cells comprise Building Regulations, Deutsches Institut für Normung (DIN) Standards, British Council for Offices guidelines, and others.

'External influencing cells' or 'antidote cells' are added regularly, to encourage recognition of the effects of the structure on the environment in which it co-exists. These antidote cells include newly introduced regulations, such as the government's guidance to dramatically reduce Carbon Emission targets.

The outer ring, the element most visible to us, is the 'Aurora' – the architectural vision; when it penetrates to the core of the molecular structure, it creates designs and environments which operate effortlessly, transcending the banal and lifting the spirits.

HOW IS THE STRUCTURE AFFECTED BY TIME?

By retracing the development of office design over time we can see a growing importance of the design briefing cells, which are reflected in both the operation of buildings and their aesthetics.

The 1920s in America saw the end of prohibition and the freedom to move from the countryside to the city. Decoration adorned the buildings in the form of plants, images of common culture and of new-found business wealth.

The Chrysler building in New York expressed the age of the motor vehicle. Giant hubcaps and shapes reminiscent of car bodywork dominated the elevations reflecting the need to promote and sell the image of the product – architecture as giant advertising hoarding.

Frank Lloyd Wright refined this to much higher levels of sophistication in the Johnson's Wax building – integrating the slick, highly-polished surfaces of the office tower with the technology of glass and the structural engineering of the communal office space.

In the 1950s, buildings like Lever House by SOM and Mies Van der Rohe's Seagram building in New York, and RMJM's New Zealand House near the north west corner of Trafalgar Square in central London, established the modern corporate office building as an architectural type. Buildings were efficient, floor plates simple, engineering systems refined and cladding systems rationalised.

The 1960s saw a major change in architectural prominence. Buildings went higher, materials became coarser and prefabrication helped deliver floor space quickly. Buildings, like skirts in this fashion-driven age, rose higher and higher.

In the UK in the late 1980s, the 'Big Bang' in the City saw a new generation of office buildings. The invasion of the Americans, as it was described in the architectural press at the time, brought with it large foot-plate buildings with clear spans of up to 18 metres, floor-to-floor heights of 4.5 metres, raised floors of 150 to 300 millimetres – all specifications aimed at a new era in banking. A move towards open plan environments accompanied an emphasis on communication and a shared drive to succeed, while the desire to demonstrate financial success led to an architectural expression dominated by the use of expensive materials such as granite and marble.

At the same time in Germany, design was one step behind that in the UK – or were they really one step ahead? The German market refused to move away from cellular office culture and the 15.4 metre wall-to-wall dimension. Klaus Daniels of HL Technik led a new generation of engineers in the environmental engineering treatment of the facade, setting new standards to reduce heat gain, using natural ventilation with minimal mechanical support systems.

Each of these projects, without knowing it at the time, reflected the standards for a new generation of office buildings.

CAN CONCLUSIONS BE DRAWN TO INFLUENCE
THE NEXT GENERATION OF OFFICE BUILDINGS?
How will the buildings of this generation reflect the age
we live in? More effort is being placed on better briefing.
Pressure is also being put on both the environment in which
we work and our physical environment. In addition, the need
for higher quality architectural design is being demanded
by clients and planners alike.

The office as an expression of our time is about to
become a new reality. This time, it will be focused on better:
· briefing
· higher environmental awareness
· more advanced technology
· greater choice of materials
· improved working conditions
· a new way of working and a new way of living.

Can we look beyond the present, so that our buildings
do more than reflect a society governed by regulations,
terrorised by fanatics, watched over by Big Brother? Will
they set the benchmarks for the next generation in terms
of sustainable design, new working methods and better use
of new technology?

Could it be that we will develop new measurement techniques
for offices that move away from necessary but rather arid
debates about net-to-gross efficiencies, intensifying
densities, and ability to handle 'churn'? Might a more accurate
determinant of business success instead measure quality
time spent both outside and inside the office?

Visually, we will move away from the glass and steel era and create environments that stimulate and inspire collaboration and creativity through the use of more domestic scale spaces and materials. This is already happening in the spaces occupied by creative small and medium-sized companies and there is a good chance that this approach to creating work environments may be adopted by larger corporate occupiers.

Will the buildings we are creating now be at ease with a new energy-aware society? Already there are clearly tensions in this respect. German engineer, Professor Dr Werner Sobek, set the industry a challenge with the development of his R129 house design, a lenticular spheroid shaped prototype developed to demonstrate energy efficiency through minimising the use of resources both in the construction of the building, the energy required over the building's lifetime and the use of recyclable construction materials.

Drawing from the progress made in materials science, nanotechnology and sensor technology, and his experience in the automotive industry, aircraft construction and space engineering, his design solutions include:
- the conservation of resources
- the reduction in the number of materials used
- the use of light recyclable materials
- no corners, an entirely round building which optimises wall to floor ratios and simplifies construction
- hollow carbon structures reducing weight and fabrication and transportation costs
- the use of futuristic technology, such as light, transparent plastic which is e-coated with switchable electronic foil.

Will the need for face-to-face communication, so successfully achieved in the European 'office-street' project types, be replaced by alternative ways of working? And will the office as an individual stand-alone building become part of an environmentally-friendly building complex, incorporating leisure, retail, offices and residential and be totally unreliant on the use of transport? Or, perhaps, we will be able to change our living environment at the flick of a switch, to a virtual office environment, and office buildings will be no more.

We are on the cusp of a new generation of work environments – whether it becomes a recognisable new age similar to those of the 1950s and the 1980s is up to the society of this age to determine. The construction industry, however, is conservative and traditional and characterised by its low level of innovation and concepts, technologies and materials, which have scarcely changed in decades.

All of the initiatives mentioned can be achieved with little help. If we are brave enough to embrace a few of the initiatives being mooted, we will create our place in history as the collective architects of a new generation of office buildings that are 'an expression of our time'.

MY FATHER WAS A PHYSICIST TURNED THEOLOGIAN AND THERE WERE MANY OCCASIONS IN MY CHILDHOOD WHEN, DURING AN EXPLANATION OF SOME CONCEPT OR PHENOMENA, HE WOULD RESORT TO PEN AND PAPER. HIS ABILITY TO USE A DIAGRAM TO ACHIEVE THE 'IGNITION' OF UNDERSTANDING SPARKED MY FASCINATION WITH THE POWER OF DIAGRAMS.

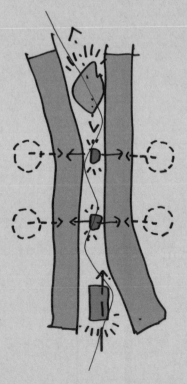

I wouldn't attribute my interest in architecture as being inspired by this early appreciation of the power of the diagram. My eyes were opened to architecture with the family exodus in the late 1960s from a 'dark satanic' Bradford to the new pedestrian precincts of 'bright and beautiful' post-war Coventry, and after marvelling at the grandeur and novelty of Basil Spence's cathedral, I bought my first set of Rotring Iso-Line pens aged 13.

It was only after starting architectural studies at university that I realised my love of diagrams (which had been sustained through my late teens by the German urbanist Walter Christaller and his theory of human settlement patterns, encountered in A Level Human Geography) had found a boundless arena in which to grow. It became obvious to me that the diagram was one of the essential tools in the creative process of architecture.

It is hard to fathom our individual architectural DNA – what makes some relish the dangerous delights of intuitive 'form-making' and why others (me included) need the surety of a reasoned, rationalised, but responsive approach.

Whilst the diagram does have a place in generating creative output across the whole spectrum of approach, it is most visible, integral and ultimately legible in architecture which is derived from the rigorous pursuit of an idea. And this idea can be encapsulated in diagrammatic form at the early stages of its genesis.

I derive great satisfaction from the 'simultaneity' of a well-crafted diagram and its ability to communicate a whole range of thoughts and responses. It provides an instant graphic language, liberated from the sequential nature of the spoken or written word. Better still, the art of producing a great diagram demands a self-conscious reductive process to omit extraneous information – a rigour which is enjoyable in itself. For me, the nature and content of the diagram evolves with the design process. The diagrammatic fun usually begins at the team selection stage, when the need to convey our appreciation of the 'project shape' to a prospective client requires the production of structure diagrams. Their design is fraught with the subtleties of appropriate line weights and page positions which reflect anticipated relationships and patterns of communication.

My typical design 'thinking' process relies on the extensive use of 'bubble' type diagrams (derivations of the Venn diagram I first discovered at junior school) which can be used to explore and establish spatial, functional and operational relationships. Here, variations in colour coding, line weight and bubble area can all convey the relative size of particular spaces, their hierarchy, interrelationships and function. For me, the bubble diagram is the best way of getting through the foothills of any project, but the final ascent towards a design solution can only be tackled from the security of the 'base camp' – the concept diagram.

Any successful project journey has, in its early stages, an exhilarating moment when, out of the mist of constraints, contradictory ideas and briefing intricacies, you suddenly reach a point where you are able to capture for the first time the essence of an idea which will guide the future

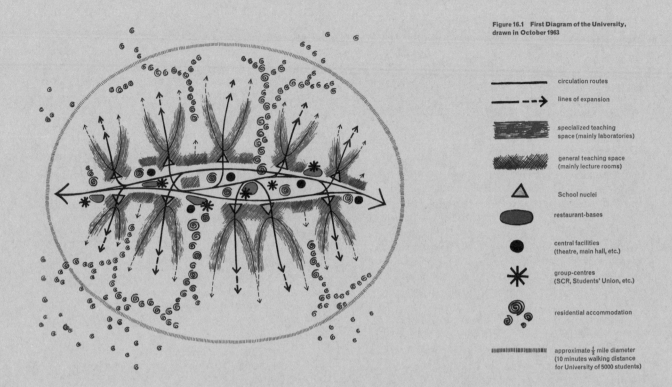

Figure 16.1   First Diagram of the University,
drawn in October 1963

circulation routes

lines of expansion

specialized teaching
space (mainly laboratories)

general teaching space
(mainly lecture rooms)

School nuclei

restaurant-bases

central facilities
(theatre, main hall, etc.)

group-centres
(SCR, Students' Union, etc.)

residential accommodation

approximate ½ mile diameter
(10 minutes walking distance
for University of 5000 students)

evolution of the scheme. The acid test of its innate robustness – and ultimate correctness – is its ability to respond and adapt to the layers of additional detail that are applied as the project proceeds.

The base camp analogy is a useful one – the concept diagram does not predetermine or predict the journey ahead. Nor does it prevent the wrong route being taken. But, when we feel as though we might be heading in the wrong direction, it allows us to revert to our core idea (back to base camp) and try again. The concept diagram becomes a tool for testing and assessing new avenues of attack and reminding ourselves of what we set out to do. The concept diagram should retain an abstract quality – declaring its potential for interpretation and acting as a signpost to the way ahead rather than offering a view of the destination.

Besides its ability to capture and test ideas, the concept diagram is probably the most powerful visual tool we have to communicate a fledgling design to our clients. Clients who might need time to assimilate and digest more formal drawings invariably enjoy and appreciate the immediacy of a well presented concept diagram.

We regularly use the concept diagram as a means of comparative analysis of similar projects, not only as part of the internal design process, but again as a means of explaining a scheme to clients.

A favourite approach, as the concept idea moves into detailed design, is to produce a series of simplified scheme drawings which communicate concise strategies in relation to the principle design ideas. These will include: spatial relationships, structural grid, servicing systems, served and servant spaces, primary circulation, fire strategy, logistics, compartmentation and arrival. These diagrams, as a 'statement of intent', act as a valuable reference point as detailed design continues and the inevitable pressure of unforeseen issues require further

design decisions to be taken – by looking back at the clear representation of our original thinking we are, once again, able to remind ourselves (and others!) of what it is we are trying to achieve.

The diagram also works effortlessly in four dimensions – the fourth dimension, of course, being time. Time can be conveyed in many ways, as in one of my favourite diagrams, which succinctly captures the patterns of movement and intensity of relationships between the components of a 1960s university campus.

As a practice, our design legacy contains a rich seam of analytical and conceptual diagrams – which are a continuous source of inspiration and delight. They display a sense of academic concentration; clarity of thinking and in many cases (such as the 'first diagram' of Bath University, 1963) a real sense of energy.

It is unfortunate that diagrams appear less and less in the architectural press – the prevalence of the slick, composed photograph in this image-hungry magazine culture has relegated the diagram to a 'gap filler'. The diagrams that do appear tend to be blatantly post-rationalised or so literal that they betray the fact that they were never a true part of the thinking process. There is something both powerful and truthful about the best diagrams that clients cannot avoid and which make architecture, and therefore architects, accessible. Striving to establish that simple communication also probably helps produce better architecture – not to mention architects.

I still seek – and find – inspiration from my 'diagrammatic heroes' – Gordon Cullen, Herman Hertzberger and Louis Kahn. And as RMJM continues to embark on projects which require us to unravel complex programmatic demands, the process of making elegant, eloquent diagrams has never been more necessary – or more enjoyable.

WE OFTEN DISCUSS AND AGREE THAT DRAWING
IS AN ESSENTIAL PART OF DESIGN, BUT WHY IS
THIS AND HOW DOES THE NATURE OF A DRAWING
PARALLEL THE DESIGN AND CONSTRUCTION OF A
BUILDING? WE PERHAPS NEED, IN THE DIGITAL AGE,
A REASONED REMINDER TO DRAW MORE OFTEN.

GRANT BLINDELL
THE SKETCH

There is a logical argument to suggest that hand drawing is losing ground. For architecture students, the digital photograph provides a more instant result, while drawing is a skill that takes too much time to refine. Higher education taints drawing with strong ideas of self-expression – a pressure on the artist to distil feelings and emotion when pen is put to paper. Drawing needs to be modernised and we need to remind ourselves of its core function and then adapt it to dovetail into the modern processes of design.

There is a growing reliance on computer-generated imagery. This is not just a reference to the hardline drawings which float from the plotters, but also the impressive computer-generated imagery that is gradually changing the focus of design, but which can also prove prescriptive.

We now plan the programme of a competition entry around the time it takes to render an image and some images are so detailed that benches and litter bins have to be designed while the massing of the scheme is still being discussed. These technology-driven requirements can place misguided emphasis on image-making at the expense of establishing strong fundamental design ideas.

Such highly persuasive imagery is understandably demanded by clients and there is, as a result, a growing link between computer presentation technology and the early design stages of a building. Has this trend begun to alter architects' skills, and has it changed the way students are equipped when they leave university? Hand-drawn examples of work in portfolios are increasingly rare. It is emphatically not the case, however, that drawing skills are no longer required. The initial

design can benefit from hand drawing, as can all subsequent meetings with clients and the documentation of a building through to on-site construction. Why is drawing important and how does its usage change from design into construction?

DESIGN – 'THOUGHT' SKETCHES

David Hockney's view was "if you can draw, even a little bit, you can express all kinds of ideas that might otherwise be lost – delights, frustration, whatever torments you or pleases you". The sketch can become much more than just describing things related to the issue at hand. It becomes something that people react to and interpret: just as the originator interprets thought into sketch, the observer interprets sketch into thought.

The ambiguity in a sketch facilitates creativity because of its need for reinterpretation on the part of the beholder. The simpler the sketch, the better. In the early stages of design, elements of ambiguity can provoke exciting alternatives as each team member (and especially the client) reads the collections of lines in a slightly different way informed by their own personal library of images and experience. The sketch becomes an essential tool in encouraging teamwork.

DETAILED DESIGN – 'BUILDING' SKETCHES

The detailed design and documentation of the building cements the concept ideas into a buildable form. The thinking ambiguity is replaced by an exploratory style which seeks method and certainty. A strong element of design is still present but now contains some definites. Materials,

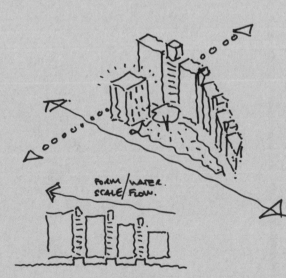

manufacturers' specific details, the technology of building, all conspire to provide a set of rules which give order to sketches produced at this stage. We no longer have a free rein.

CONSTRUCTION – 'COMMUNICATION' SKETCHES
The design becomes increasingly stable as the process progresses to the point when construction begins. At this stage sketching becomes much more about communication of the particular between the design and the people building the project. It must be clear with no ambiguity. The drawing style and accompanying language change to ensure complete transfer of information.

The language that explains sketches at these varying stages alters in parallel with the ambiguity of the drawing. At the early design stages phrases such as, "well it may not be like this, but what if…?" allow other members of the team room for interpretation, whereas later things are tied down in a far more confident "it is like this…" manner. The role of drawing in design has a distinct relationship to language. It is a base level skill we develop from childhood.

If we accept the reasons why hand-drawn communication is so critical, we should ensure its role is protected by adapting to the changing techniques that now surround us.

It is during the initial phases of a project that advancing technology has had the most impact. And it is in these stages that the role of the sketch has most need for adaptation. Computers do not purvey ambiguity, but all projects must go through a stage of ambiguity to achieve resolution. Premature

resolution may be a mirage. Computers are a digital medium that deliver an instant 'hardline'. It is very difficult, and time-consuming, to get an emotional image from a computer. Software advances are closing the gap but maybe the move should be the other way in order not to lose the vital process of thought-to-paper.

The level of completeness of images which now appear at such early stages of projects suggests the building has been detailed – but this is clearly not the case and there will still be a lot of detail to work through. To help avoid disappointments, we should adapt the types of sketches to inform and aid the visualisation of the design. The three types of sketch mentioned are now all used at the early design stages. The thinking sketch is still used to express thought and engage others in collaborative design. The building sketches are now used to think about how the building will fit together to further inform the visualisers. The communication sketches are employed in the final presentations to clearly distil the core ideas.

A benefit of this closing gap between the sketch and the computer-generated image is the removal of the pressure to develop highly-tuned drafting skills. Designers can be free-flowing with their sketches in the knowledge that the precision and control will be injected at a different stage. By clearly defining the role of the sketch, we can more purely utilise its key benefits. To encourage its use constructively, we should understand our drawn languages more clearly so that our technology emulates them more sympathetically. Equally, designers must use and understand technology to enhance our established communication methods.

URBAN DESIGN OFFERS US THE OPPORTUNITY TO ANALYSE, EVOLVE AND CREATE THE CONTEXTS IN WHICH WE LIVE AND WORK.

NATHAN WARD
URBAN DESIGN, 'A DEVELOPMENTAL APPROACH'

RMJM's role as urban designers is to establish a framework that will support the opportunities for future vitality within new or existing urban environments. We synthesise the social, environmental, and economic factors that form the basis of our cultural identity, in order to provide vibrant and sustainable urban environments.

The work RMJM carries out in diverse urban contexts often involves a wide cross-section of stakeholders, organisations, politicians, and professionals, all of whom become part of the creative process.

There are many technical and financial aspects to this process, however it is understanding what generates the unique identity of each environment that is fundamental to successful urban design. Our design proposals provide definition to the form and function of an environment, but we cannot imbue them with a 'sense of place'. Environments require habitation for that.

URBAN DESIGN – ARCHITECTURE OF THE IN-BETWEEN
It is through perception that a 'sense of place' is developed. The process of perception allows us to establish a relationship between ourselves and the things around us. There are two components to this process: the plastic physical world which can be changed and which we as designers readily utilise; the other being the immaterial or non-physical, the 'perceptual' component. This is something we can manipulate through design, but which we cannot prescribe.

The immaterial element of an environment provides meaning and identity to a context. If you were to experience an object and bring no background knowledge to it, you would simply experience a three-dimensional form in space isolated from the world around it by a lack of relative meaning. Our work aims to provide proposals that provide for both functional requirements and which are rooted in their cultural context.

Where do the physical and the immaterial sides of our environment meet?

The British philosopher John Locke, 1632–1704, held the view that there is nothing in the intellect that was not previously in the senses. This simple statement brings together the physical and the immaterial, and introduces a common ground of human experience between the two, where our knowledge

and experience of environments helps us understand the identity of a particular location.

Lev Semenovich Vygotsky, 1896 – 1934, a Soviet psychologist whose work was published after his death and then quickly suppressed, proposed a 'developmental approach' to psychology which can provide a useful basis for expanding on Locke's view. Vygotsky proposed that there are three key elements to this developmental approach:

· Phylogenesis (biological evolution)
· Sociogenesis (cultural history)
· Ontogenesis (individual development)[1].

These describe a way of understanding how we perceive the world around us, through the experiences we encounter, the cultural context in which they are placed, and our physical or biological needs, all of which combine to form a unique set of experiences that colour our perception of environments.

Urban design inhabits a position dualistic between the physical world of things and the immaterial world of perception. It is the processes we employ as urban designers that will affect how we successfully deliver a balanced environment.

LOST IN FOUR-DIMENSIONAL SPACE
In delivering an urban design proposal we are not only required to fully understand the contexts in which we work but also to be conversant with the characteristics of our medium. This environmental medium in which human activity takes place, is characterised by a series of components:

· Location (physical – site/internal characteristics)
· Uniqueness (ensemble of particular elements)
· Circulation (interconnection and spatial interactions)
· Locality (context and setting in relation to other places)
· Evolution (historical and cultural change)
· Meaning (beliefs, interpretation and understanding)[2].

The concept of a fourth dimension – time – is implicit here and in Vygotsky's developmental approach. The link between time and space provides us with an understanding of how we can deliver environments that are easily inhabited, are able to grow and adapt, to incorporate richness and meaning beyond their physical structure.

This developmental or evolutionary process may be found in planned settlements, such as Edinburgh's New Town, Inveraray, or the grids of Glasgow's Merchant City, New York or Chicago. In these places, an underlying structure has remained even though they have evolved and adapted over time, each developing a unique sense of place related to the social, environmental and the economic forces that drive their development.

RICHNESS OF CITIES
Richness is a quality successful urban environments have in abundance; Michel Foucault proposed a theory of Heterogeneity (the quality of being made of many different elements, forms, kinds, or individuals), where space is thoroughly imbued with meaning and richness, and not homogeneous, without variation, or having similar parts throughout. Foucault suggested that heterotopias pervade space, rather as the fourth dimension does, involving multiplicities of scale, linkages and degrees of openness: "In other words, we do not live in a kind of void, inside of which we could place individuals and things. We do not live inside a void that could be coloured with diverse shades of light, we live inside a set of relations that delineates sites which are irreducible to one another and absolutely not superimposable on one another." [3]

Today there are many effects that limit heterogeneity, under the guise of diversity, for example globalising influences push toward an 'a-spatial society', (a term that is used to describe the non-spatial, i.e. the erosion of a link between locality and information seen in the notion of 'cyber-space', for example), instead of celebrating uniqueness and richness of a place.[4] It also occurs in the creation of pseudo-public space where there can be an overt underlying control mechanism or a lack of ownership or control. Examples of how dehumanising an imbalance in control is can be found in the lack of success of mass social housing schemes, such as Hulme Crescents in Manchester.

In considering richness in our work we can foster vibrancy in an urban environment with the potential for the inclusion of various activities – i.e., places to work and homes to live in. However, there is another function apart from home and work, a 'third place'. This is defined in a book by Ray Oldenburg entitled *The Great Good Place: Cafes, Coffee Shops, Bookstores, Bars, Hair Salons, and Other Hangouts at the Heart of a Community.*

The 'third place', as Oldenburg puts it, is the 'city's raison d'être' and can breathe life into the 'in-between' times and spaces. The importance of a space apart from work and home is also suggested by architectural writer and teacher Katherine Shonfield, in an influential Demos report published in 1998 entitled *The Richness of Cities: urban policy in a new landscape.* Among other things this describes the importance of varied spaces that allow a "spatial democracy of shared experience".[5] The shared experience of our public spaces expresses an important part of who we are and how we define ourselves to others.

THE ARTWORK OF DEVELOPMENT AND EVOLUTION
The definition of environments through the enclosure, manipulation, provision and programming of space can provide opportunities and guide how environments may be inhabited. However, to be successful in the long term, the work we carry out has to foster adaptability, uniqueness, variety, richness, and activity, because without them our urban environments would lack cultural meaning. Complexity in an urban context is something we should celebrate; the understanding of how the processes of perception and place-making works is fundamental to the success of producing new urban environments.

In evolving and creating urban environments RMJM's holistic approach is not unlike that of the De Stijl movement's 'total art work' or *Gesamtkunstwerk*; although our approach is more fluid, site-specific and adaptable, somewhat less deterministic, and could be described as *Entwicklungskunstwerk* or 'the artwork of development and evolution'.

[1] C Bourassa, Stephen, "A paradigm for Aesthetics".

[2] Relph, E, "Place and Placelessness".

[3] Foucault, Michel, "Of Other Spaces", *Heterotopias*.

[4] Peponis, John, "Space, culture and urban design", *Ekistics*.

[5] Shonfield, Katherine, "The Richness of Cities: urban policy in a new landscape".

THE PERSONAL COMPUTER MAY HAVE TRANSFORMED
THE WAY WE DRAW AND COMMUNICATE OUR
DESIGNS, BUT THERE IS STILL A LARGELY UNTAPPED
POTENTIAL TO USE COMPUTER GRAPHICS AS A TOOL
DURING THE FIRST PHASES OF THE DESIGN PROCESS.

JONATHAN MESSER
THE FUTURE OF COMPUTER VISUALISATION

Computer modelling can play a larger role via applications
that aid and amplify the creative process.

THE COMPUTER AS A DRAFTING TOOL

Over the last decade, the widespread acceptance of
computer technology has had a significant impact throughout
the construction industry. In architecture, as in other fields,
the initial uptake of computerisation was generally driven by
the desire to free humans from tedious and mundane tasks.
Computer Aided Design (CAD) software has revolutionised the
drafting process, enabling quick and accurate drawing and
simple modification as designs develop, at the same time
streamlining the flow of information between consultants.
Increasingly, CAD systems also have the ability to exchange
quantitative data, greatly simplifying the analysis and
construction of proposed designs.

THE COMPUTER AS A COMMUNICATION TOOL

As designers, having the ability to present our proposals to
clients, statutory authorities and members of the public in
a convincing and visually accurate way brings us tremendous
advantages. Modelling and rendering systems have proven
to be invaluable aids, speeding up the evolution of ideas while
keeping everyone involved and informed throughout.

We have the technology and ability to communicate the
aesthetics, light, rhythm and proportion of an architectural
design. At present, we tend to use this technology near the
conclusion of a larger design process, leaving the full potential
of its use as a design tool largely untapped.

THE COMPUTER AS A DESIGN TOOL

Architectural design is an iterative, visual process – one that
involves thinking and exploring in pictorial or symbolic
representations. The traditional tools of architectural design –
pencil and paper, cardboard, clay and wire – have a common
set of properties. Each is pliant, flexible and forgiving. By their
nature they encourage exploration and experimentation.
Similarly, if used appropriately, visualisations can be open-
ended, informal and personal, encouraging exploration and
iteration, rather than being rigid and precise and focusing
on accurate specification of geometric relationships.

It should not be the case that most of the artistic and
intellectual challenges of an architectural design have already
been resolved by the time the visualiser sits down in front of
a computer. Modelling can be used not only to produce images
for marketing or persuading planners, but also throughout the
design process, from day one, allowing designers to explore,
assess and refine their ideas, in the same way balsa models
have been used in the past. The process of creating a well-
designed virtual space is, in essence, the same process that
leads to well-designed physical space; starting with
establishing goals, developing the concept, then collaboratively
designing and re-designing the environment. Speculative
visualisations are essential to the creative process. Images
rarely exist in the mind fully-formed and detailed, waiting only
to be transferred to a sheet of paper.

Initially, with the use of simple 'user friendly' programmes, we
are able to explore ideas as loose, diagrammatic 3-D models,
which stimulate the imagination, test initial thoughts and
concepts and generate a series of alternatives. As a design
concept is developed and clarified, the 3-D models employed
to study the idea also become more definitive and refined,
until the proposal is crystallised and presented for evaluation
and implementation.

The role of visualisation, during the speculative design
process, is to allow an immediate snapshot of ideas for
examination and revision and to provide a record of the
exploration process for later review. Speculative models
are, therefore, different in spirit and purpose from the
definitive presentation media that architects use to
accurately represent and communicate a fully formed design
to others. The biggest benefit and greatest potential that
computer visualisations can bring are when they are used
as a tool to aid the design process and produce better
buildings as a result.

RMJM'S AMBITION IS TO CREATE THOUGHTFUL,
POETIC, CONTEMPORARY DESIGN THAT IS RICH
IN MEANING AND HAS RELEVANCE TO PEOPLE.

PAUL STALLAN
CELEBRATING THE BRITISH WEATHER – THE CONCEPTUAL AND THE CLIMATIC

We seek a confident, indigenous, regional architecture
nurtured from our unique climate and context, an
architecture that responds to our variable climate, that
is more than merely technically proficient but is thoughtful
and conceptual, which does not require a blue Mediterranean
sky to show it at its most tectonic and dramatic.

What is there, though, to celebrate about our 'great
British weather' that might inform architecture? And how,
conceptually and visually, can a culture reflect the poetry
of our climate and our unique situation through our art and
architecture? Surely the weather has an influence on our
national character, but how can architects and designers
celebrate this?

Imagine being inside a cloud. We would perhaps consider
an architecture that is more hermetic and introvert; an
architecture that protects us from the cold and wet – more
interior than exterior. This might seem ridiculous, but it helps
us to understand the contrast between a visual and a sensual
experience of a damp and moist world. As the American boy
who arrived in Scotland for the first time asked, "Daddy, why
is the sky so low?"

It is clear to anyone who has returned to the UK after
travelling or working elsewhere in the world that climate
affects our collective culture and our individual psyche. Both
'climate' and 'place' fundamentally influence and shape how we
engage with the world and our immediate environment. Whole
cultures are imbued with characteristics that are a result of
geography and location.

From a personal perspective, my experience of living in Glasgow
as a child and adult has given me a certain relationship and
outlook on the world. Being not only Scottish, but having
worked and lived in Glasgow, once the second city of the
British Empire and Scotland's industrial centre, I carry some

of the city's baggage, which has inevitably informed my critical thinking and approach to design.

To elaborate on everyday experiences and how they inform our attitudes to architecture, French architect Bernard Tschumi describes his approach as "an architecture that has less to do with the experience of forms but rather forms of experience". It is not what you think about architecture, but how you think that informs your relationship with architecture.

Tschumi's viewpoint seems relevant. Reinforcing positive experiences for people in architecture through the introduction of meaning, reason, layers, spatial complexity, thresholds and drama, we can create a more involving design that interacts and stimulates people beyond just visual experience.

An example of experiencing form, compared to a form of experience, that has helped me clarify this concept of a 'distant architecture' versus an 'in the round architecture' is the marked difference between watching theatre in front of a traditional proscenium arch and watching a performance in the round, where the audience surrounds the action. You can just look in a traditional theatre; whereas in-the-round, you feel more physically engaged in the action. For me this is the difference between just looking at architecture and participating in it.

I would argue we have a more intimate or in-the-round relationship with architecture in the UK compared to sunnier climates for the simple reason that we spend more time indoors or under cover. In this respect developing and exploring a contemporary architectural language and urbanism that is less about shapes and forms and more to do with spaces and places and experience becomes more relevant.

To achieve the kind of architecture which suits our climate and our culture better, perhaps we have to challenge and push the potential of our buildings to develop a more dynamic contextual and spatial architecture. Our building envelopes must respond in more imaginative and inclusive ways and be more site specific. We need buildings that keep the rain out and the heat in, but we also need buildings that are not wholly introvert and private.

Considering our building envelopes and elevations, it is helpful to refer to the modern movement across Europe and how it expounded the reduction of the material thickness of the load bearing wall in favour of more industrial construction techniques. This modernist functional principle had a significant impact on the character and traditional view of our national architecture.

In the last 50 years, buildings enclosed in manufactured glass, concrete and metal panel systems have dramatically changed our townscapes and cities. Technically, however, modern buildings now have walls that are paper-thin. The UK, like other places across the world, has many characterless glass and brick buildings where the particulars and differences of their context do not influence them in the slightest. The challenge is to try and recapture 'difference' in architecture without resorting to literal references or pastiche; to celebrate the local without being slave to the building systems available, but rather to mould them to support a dynamic and responsive architecture that can be both open and closed to the world. Our buildings have to be more exciting to engage us in a colder climate. They cannot be merely about keeping the rain off, nor should they be designed as though they belonged somewhere else.

DELIVERING HIGH QUALITY BUILDINGS AND URBAN
DEVELOPMENTS IS A COMPLEX PROCESS, WITH
SHARED AMBITIONS AND GOOD INTENTIONS UNDER
PRESSURE FROM THE PRACTICALITIES INVOLVED
IN PRESENTING A SUCCESSFUL PROJECT ON TIME,
TO BUDGET.

LUCY ANDREW
RMJM AND ECOHOMES

Wider ethical considerations – related to social or
environ-mental sustainability – tend to get squeezed, despite
all the regulations and initiatives intended to ensure the
elements that make up our built environment (homes,
workplaces and infrastructure) meet these criteria. But these
pressures can produce the best and most creative solutions.

Finding practical tools that enable all of the partners in a
project to understand and buy into a core agenda at the
earliest briefing stage increases the likelihood that the team
will fight to retain features in a project and ensure the phrase
'sustainable communities' means something practical beyond
the political arena.

EcoHomes is the Building Research Establishment's
Environmental Assessment Method (BREEAM) for domestic
buildings. It is a tool that RMJM has used successfully to
help clients to understand the holistic nature of a project's
environmental impact, and to enable clients to commit to
practical strategies for delivering better buildings. It
generates an environmental rating, using a points system,
for all domestic buildings based on the widest possible
criteria. A project's energy use, water consumption, land use,
material consumption and waste, building users' transport
requirements and associated pollution, are given simple point
scores along with wider health and well-being considerations
such as day-lighting and acoustic performance.

Much of RMJM's recent portfolio of domestic projects and
urban masterplans has been well suited to the EcoHomes
process. High-density urban projects, often built on
brownfield sites with a generous provision of public transport
links and amenities, already rate highly on the EcoHomes
system without the need to incorporate extraordinary
environmentally friendly features. Increasingly, high standards
for building envelope performance, which tighten almost
annually, have pushed transport-related emissions to the
forefront of the energy saving agenda.

What is commendable about the EcoHomes system is
that it shifts the discussion away from the stereotypical
preconceptions of green building and helps clients to
understand that projects needn't be made of straw and
powered by windmills to contribute to an environmentally
and socially sustainable environment.

By focusing instead on high urban densities with well-
integrated local amenities and incorporating simple measures
to achieve super insulation levels, EcoHomes is proving to be
a successful system that locks in environmental ambitions at
the briefing stage of a project. Rather than achieving your
green credentials through a range of accessories that can
easily be jettisoned along the way, the EcoHomes assessment
enables you to modify your strategy at the outset – creating
a strong, pre-agreed foundation to build from.

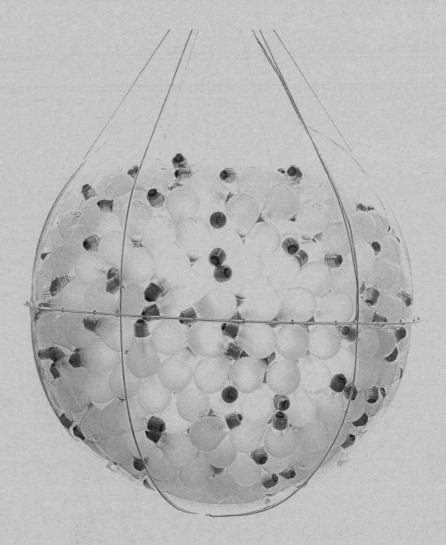

For clients and users alike, it demystifies much of the discussion surrounding sustainability, and moves away from the messianic and often puritanical tone of earlier pronouncements by the green lobby. If we are serious about achieving obligations to international environmental agreements, whilst at the same time providing communities which support a higher quality of life, we must find ways of encouraging the construction industry to participate enthusiastically rather than being dragged along grudgingly. The EcoHomes approach is more encouraging in this respect.

Consumers are more and more looking to buy environmentally friendly products and investors, similarly, recognise the added value of an ethical portfolio. Few are prepared to compromise on their standard of living and investment return, however. This creates an exciting new challenge for designers to innovate and reduce the environmental impact of new and existing developments whilst maintaining, or better still improving, our quality of life.

As competition amongst new developments gathers pace, the EcoHomes stamp should prove to be a worthwhile investment for homes which consume less and offer more. It is also a method of generating a design discipline for a scheme at the outset which helps to reduce risk for the client by fixing specification parameters that might otherwise have been subject to change and to enhance a development's appeal to consumers.

ECOHOMES – A SUMMARY FOR CLIENTS
- Part of the Building Research Establishment's BREEAM family of eco-assessment methods, EcoHomes rates the environmental qualities of both new and renovated homes using independent assessors, rated on a scale of Pass, Good, Very Good and Excellent.
- The scheme rewards developers who improve the environmental performance of a scheme through good design rather than expensive capital cost items. Ratings are carried out at the design stage and a post-construction review can also be carried out, which provides a separate certificate.
- The Design Stage assessment process is carried out in three phases, including a specification assessment, a house type assessment and a development assessment, which assesses a site's ecological value and transport issues. Phases one and two can be carried out without reference to a specific site.
- The EcoHomes publication and the Green Guide to Housing Specification can be bought online at www.brebookshop.com

QUICK REWIND: THE LATE TWENTIETH CENTURY AND ARCHITECTURE, THE SUPPOSED 'MOTHER OF THE ARTS', HAS FAILED ITS CHILDREN – VERY TRAUMATIC. IT TRIED ITS BEST BUT THE KIDS TURNED ON IT.

PAUL STALLAN
ATTITUDE, ART AND ARCHITECTURE

The trauma of banal architecture and featureless new towns spawned nostalgia and disillusion. Punk, fashion, music, football, community architecture, visual art; these are some of the many ways people responded to the condition of the built environment and to make sense of the postmodern world they inhabited.

Against the backdrop of failed council estates and commercial house builder sprawl, motorway intersections and the decline of our city centres, along with the departure of industry for more amenable economies, 'Brit Art' and the 'creative industries' fought back and took the world by storm.

The currency of Britain's future would seem to be 'ideas'. Not since the Punk explosion of the mid-1970s has the UK been as creative, energetic and interesting. It is, allegedly, the most fashionable place in the world. The creative boom and the reawakening of the public's interest in art has not been restricted to London, but has also developed in other major cities like Manchester, Glasgow and Belfast.

Energised by the tension and angst of entering a new millennium, provocative conceptual and environmental art has taken radical cynicism, irony and social comment into mainstream culture. Think of the pop group, the K Foundation, burning a million pounds on a beach, the Sensation art exhibition at the Royal Academy (no less) or Tracey Emin's bed.

Now press PLAY. Brits have 'attitude' and are seen internationally as clever and interesting. Thatcher's children have grown up and are tough, talented, dysfunctional and commercial. Artists like Damien Hirst or Glaswegian video-artist Douglas Gordon and other British artists have written and continue to write a whole new chapter for the visual art world in the twenty-first century. Conceptual art has exploded in the UK. Artists are collaborating with scientists, filmmakers, dancers and the public, seeking out new ways of communicating.

The exciting thing for architects is to be inspired by and collaborate with our artistic cousins. A new generation of visual artists are responding to the environment in ways architects have never dreamed of. Art is being subversive,

playful, everyday, challenging – basically reframing and replaying people's experiences and environment.

Artists are embracing meaning and ideas and not just visual form. This is something architects might learn more from – how as architects we can make our buildings more relevant. As Le Corbusier said, "Architecture without art is mere building."

UK architects have begun to reflect and embrace with confidence a new conceptual architectural practice to compliment the success of the UK's contemporary visual arts. Small and large practices alike are developing and investing in thoughtful process-orientated architecture that is carefully and intelligently satisfying an understandably suspicious British public.

Architects are increasingly responsive to the environment, while clients are gaining confidence in the potential of 'conceptual architecture' which embraces the potential of the specific local and parochial conditions.

Excited about the potential of a more conceptual architecture, RMJM is experimenting and exploring ways to elevate our immediate environments and introducing into it layers of meaning; through text and graphics, sound installations, colour, lighting, local landscape and innovation in materials and textures. RMJM has the only integrated art commissioning service within an architectural practice in the UK. The team strategically assesses opportunities for contemporary artists within architectural schemes, secures funding and implements the artists' commission. Since its creation in 2001 the team has worked with internationally-acclaimed artists including Kenny Hunter, Peter McCaughey, Tracey McKenna and Toby Paterson on initiatives including education, residential and urban design projects.

UK architects – architecture as a whole – is embracing a 'more than architecture' approach, a collaborative, more inclusive working practice, which is long overdue and represents a healing of the rift that some of the failures in British Modernism wrought.

TONY KETTLE
WORKING WITH ARTISTS

As architects today, collaborating with artists is not only about installing artworks within our buildings but this collaboration can also extend to the actual design of the building.

The separation of art and architecture is only a recent phenomenon dating from the eighteenth century when fine art became detached. Previously, there were no boundaries and the architect and artist were one. Nowadays, architects are concerned with justifying everything in the building, on the other hand artists often set out not to justify what they do, they are almost in opposition. By working with an artist, the architect is able to fully explore freedom of thought and therefore consider issues at a conceptual level from first principles. Surely it is by designing from first principles that real innovation is possible.

The relevance of an artist's work to a particular design is vital if the collaboration is to work. Scale is not that relevant, it is the design thought process that is key. Architects are used to collaborating everyday as part of a design team, while artists tend to work singularly so the choice of artist requires careful consideration.

RMJM's recent experience of collaboration with artists in the design process has, overall, proved to be very positive. Our collaboration with Scottish artist Karen Forbes on the City Palace Tower in Moscow grew from a shared interest in the symbolic, the hidden messages within objects and the particular brief, which called for something more than a conventional commercial response.

Our interest in promoting this type of collaboration led us to establish the RMJM Award for Art and Architecture which was launched at Edinburgh College of Art. Each year, we set a brief to undergraduate students of architecture, drawing and painting, and sculpture. They are asked to respond to a place through a collaborative working process and present their ideas as a team. The success of the award has been tremendous – not only does the collaboration between the students from different disciplines produce inspiring and highly creative solutions but each student leaves the competition richer for the collaboration.

THE UK POPULATION IS AGEING. IN RESPONSE TO
THIS DEMOGRAPHIC SHIFT A GROWING NUMBER OF
DEVELOPERS ARE SPECIALISING IN THE PROVISION
OF RETIREMENT APARTMENTS.

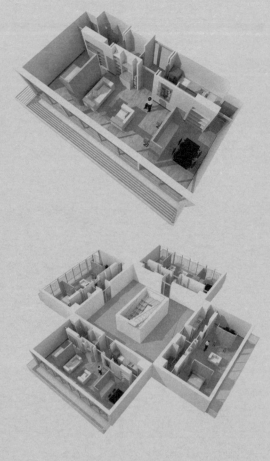

PATRICK WILSON
THE CONCEPTUAL COMPACT APARTMENT MODULE

RMJM has invested in research and development work in this
rapidly growing market to explore the specific design issues
that housing for an ageing population entails.

Many people approaching retirement want to release equity
in existing property. The aspiration is usually to move to
smaller accommodation, close to transport links and
amenities. Many of the mainstream, new-build residential
developments rarely appeal, as these attract younger people.

The housing provided by specialist developers has more
to offer: they are usually exclusively available to people of
retirement age offering increased security and incorporating
care facilities, on-call wardens and common social spaces.
Also, the sites are chosen for their urban location providing
easy access to local amenities and transport.

For the developer, this means acquiring small town centre
sites with high land values, which require high density schemes
using efficient designs to produce a viable development. One
major advantage (from the developer's point of view and the
environment's) of a dedicated retirement development is a
reduction in the need for car parking. Depending on the area
and the local authority, this can be as low as 50 per cent –
i.e. one car space for every two homes. This presents an
opportunity to achieve a higher than normal value from a site.

DEMOGRAPHICS
The number of the population over 50 is projected to rise
from the current 20 million to 25 million within 20 years.
By 2020, the population over 50 will comprise half the
adult population.

The number of people aged 65 and over is currently nine
million and is projected to reach 12.5 million by 2020. The
rate of people aged 75 and over is expected to increase
even faster.

In contrast, the numbers in younger age groups are expected
to decline, with the population of pensionable age projected
to exceed the number of under-16s by 2007.

There is a perception that the market demands a postmodern
Victorian or Edwardian pastiche architectural style, and that
is what is generally available. The common model is either a
one or two-bedroom apartment, and in order to achieve
affordability they tend to be smaller than mainstream

developments would provide. The result is often uninspiring
and confined and unlikely to meet the taste of the generation
soon to be approaching retirement which bought much of its
furniture at IKEA.

RMJM has developed a design for a contemporary apartment
module as an attractive alternative to the architectural
pastiche styles available and which would also create added
value for the developer through its efficient and imaginative
use of space. This conceptual compact apartment module is
designed to achieve much more from its 50 square metres
than current standards dictate.

SIMPLE, STYLISH, FUNCTIONAL, RATIONAL
The five by ten metre plan provides an entrance into the
centre of the apartment. A 'service' zone containing kitchen,
bathroom and utility space runs the length of the rear of the
module, with the living, dining and sleeping spaces all opening
onto a fully-glazed elevation. A 'functioning' wall separates
these two zones accommodating wardrobe space in the
bedroom(s), an entertainment zone for TV, stereo, shelving
etc., in the living room and display cabinet/cupboard for the
dining area/second bedroom.

The division of the living space into bedroom, living and dining
areas is highly adaptable. Sliding partitioning and openings
throughout allow the apartment to be as enclosed or as open-
plan as desired – providing light and spacious accommodation.

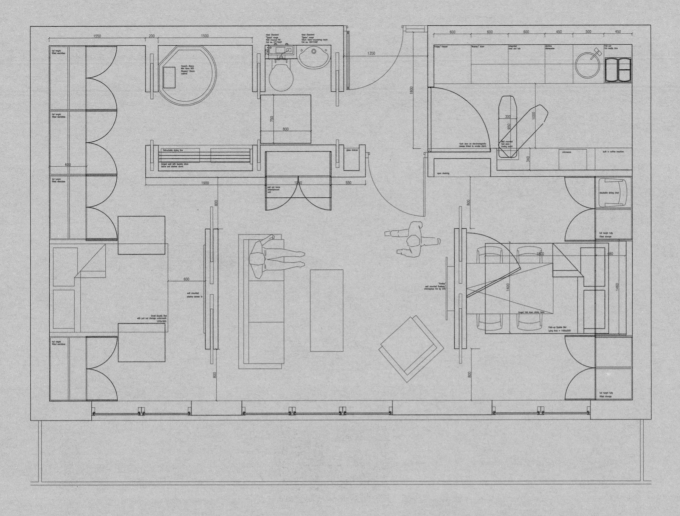

Space-saving fixtures and fittings and additional storage are integrated into the fabric of the apartment, bringing an added level of functionality and further adding to the perception of volume and space. Modern fire engineering solutions can be incorporated to ensure the open-plan approach meets fire and building regulations.

BUILDABILITY

The plan form lends itself well to any number of multi-storey configurations. The module works as well in a four-storey urban block as it does a multi-storey tower, or even as a single unit 'cottage'. These logical configurations also present the opportunity to adopt the most rational structural solutions, including the possibility of prefabrication. Cladding material options are virtually endless, giving the unit the potential to be considered for a wide range of sites where we are required to integrate sensitively into different and varied contexts.

ECONOMY AND VALUE

The simple, rational form dictates buildability and, therefore, the potential for a highly economical construction process. Where reduced parking requirements allow, there is the opportunity to achieve a very high yield from smaller urban sites. The compact design and imaginative use of space, furniture and fixtures potentially offer afford-ability within the housing market whilst maximising development yield.

THE FUTURE

Precedents for 'compact living' solutions that address the lack of affordable housing in cities and maximise land use in dense urban areas have often aimed at developing single person dwellings in the form of compact 'studio' arrangements. RMJM's proposal presents a highly efficient compact apartment to meet the demands of the growing retirement market. It provides comfortable, two-person accommodation within an adaptable layout that is capable of providing additional living, dining, study or sleeping accommodation not normally offered by current compact living solutions.

The modular nature of the apartment in different block configurations presents the opportunity to substitute one or more apartments for support, ancillary and social spaces to create a community as sheltered and secure as required for each development.

BANGKOK
66 Q HOUSE ASOKE, 14TH FLOOR
SUKHUMVIT 21 RD, KLONGTOEY NUA
WATTANA, BANGKOK 10110
THAILAND
T +662 2642130
F +662 2642136
E thailand@rmjm.com

BEIJING
A608 JIANWAI SOHO
NO.39 EAST 3RD RING ROAD
CHAOYANG DISTRICT
BEIJING 100022
CHINA
T +8610 5869 8296/97/98
F +8610 5869 8295
E beijing@rmjm.com

CAMBRIDGE
THE OLD RECTORY
CHURCH LANE
FULBOURN
CAMBRIDGE CB1 5EP
UNITED KINGDOM
T +44 1223 881 881
F +44 1223 881 611
E cambridge@rmjm.com

DUBAI
DUBAI INTERNATIONAL
CONVENTION CENTRE
PO BOX 6126
DUBAI
UNITED ARAB EMIRATES
T +9714 331 4120
F +9714 331 4199
E dubai@rmjm.com

EDINBURGH
10 BELLS BRAE
EDINBURGH EH4 3BJ
UNITED KINGDOM
T +44 131 225 2532
F +44 131 226 5117
E edinburgh@rmjm.com

GLASGOW
SKYPARK SP1
8 ELLIOT PLACE
GLASGOW G3 8EP
UNITED KINGDOM
T +44 141 275 3410
F +44 141 275 3411
E glasgow@rmjm.com

LONDON
83 PAUL STREET
LONDON EC2A 4UT
UNITED KINGDOM
T +44 20 7549 8900
F +44 20 7250 3131
E london@rmjm.com

HONG KONG
33RD FLOOR
COSCO TOWER
GRAND MILLENNIUM PLAZA
183 QUEEN'S ROAD CENTRAL
HONG KONG
T +852 2548 1698
F +852 2547 6386/2803 0403
E hongkong@rmjm.com

SHANGHAI
SUITE NO.2502
SHANGHAI TIAN AN CENTER
338 NANJING WEST ROAD
SHANGHAI
200003 CHINA
T +86 021 6372 9005/9003/9006
F +86 021 6372 9002
E shanghai@rmjm.com

SINGAPORE
137 TELOK AYER STREET
#03-01
SINGAPORE 068602
T +65 6327 4681
F +65 6327 4951
E singapore@rmjm.com

ACKNOWLEDGEMENTS

RMJM would like to thank the following people for their invaluable input to this publication: Duncan McCorquodale at Black Dog Publishing, Rhona Findlay and everyone at Third Eye Design, Simon Platt, Lee Mallett, Sir Andrew Derbyshire, Ken Feakes and Miles Glendinning. Thanks to those from the practice who contributed an essay; Lucy Andrew, Grant Blindell, Tony Kettle, Juliet Landler, Jonathan Messer, Colin Moses, Dana Raydan, Nathan Ward, Roger Whiteman, Peter Williams and Patrick Wilson. Thanks also to everyone who assisted with the sourcing of the wealth of material for the publication and to all RMJM colleagues, past and present, who contributed to the success of the projects featured. A special thanks to Paul Stallan and Claire Scott for successfully managing this project. Finally, thanks to our non-executive directors for their counsel and to all our clients for their continued support, vision and enthusiasm.

IMAGES
© Fayer 4
© Henk Snoek/RIBA Library Photographs Collection 13, 16, 18, 21 [right], 23 [left]
© Henk Snoek 14, 20 [left], 21 [left], 96 [bottom], 151 [bottom]
© Sam Lambert/RIBA Library Photographs Collection 20 [right]
© Chris Gascoigne/VIEW 24, 30, 48 [third row, far right], 97 [bottom right], 119, 121 [top], 121 [second from left], 121 [second from right], 124, 126, 147, 148 [left]
© Andrew Lee 26, 31, 48 [fourth row, far right], 49 [first row, right], 68, 69 [images 1,2 and 3], 70, 71, 113, 129
© Peter Cook/VIEW 27, 127 [top row, second from left]
© Hufton + Crow 28, 29, 96 [top right], 97 [bottom left], 171
© Janeanne Gilchrist, Unit Photographic 46, 47, 48 [third row left], 48 [sixth row, left], 49 [third row, left], 49 [fourth row, left], 49 [fifth row, second from right], 49 [sixth row, left], 50, 51, 74, 75, 100, 101, 122, 123
Paul Stallan 48 [fourth row, third from left], 49 [first row, left]
© Keith Hunter/arcblue.com 54, 55 [top and second row left], 94, 95, 121 [bottom left], 146 [left]
© Ryan McGoverne 60 [main image], 61
© David Churchill/arcaid.co.uk 69 [image 4]
© Matt Laver 97 [top left], 97 [top right], 133, 146 [right], 149 [top left]
© Timothy Soar 107, 135, 137, 148 [right]
© Nick Guttridge/VIEW 127 [top left and top right], 149 [bottom left]
© Mark Noë 151 [top]
© Gavan Goulder 172, 173

OTHER IMAGE CREDITS
Image courtesy of the Scottish Mining Museum, 52 [top]
Reproduced from the collection of the late Mr William Harrison, 52 [bottom left]
Chain Pier, Brighton – Constable © Tate, London 2006, 77
Images provided by the Glasgow Digital Library at the Centre for Digital Library Research (CDLR), University of Strathclyde, 82
Cold Kiss © Hulton Archive/Getty Images 90
Courtesy of Sir Robert Matthew's family, 138, 139, 142
© Digital Vision/Getty Images, 153
'Bulb of Light' by Joakim Fihn courtesy of the artist, 165

Black Dog Publishing Limited
Unit 4.4 Tea Building
56 Shoreditch High Street
London
E1 6JJ

Tel: +44 (0)20 7613 1922
Fax: +44 (0)20 7613 1944
Email: info@bdp.demon.co.uk

www.bdpworld.com

British Library Cataloguing-in-Publication Data.

A CIP record for this book is available from the British Library.

ISBN 10: 1 904772 59 5
ISBN 13: 9 781904 772590

THIRDEYEDESIGN

architecture art design
fashion history photography
theory and things

black dog
publishing

www.bdpworld.com